Table of Contents

Who makes the list?

Compiling any "Best of" or "Worst of" list throws up a number of challenges for the author, and that is particularly true when the selection criteria is not easily quantifiable. Now wait a moment, I hear you say, surely the worst serial killers are those with the highest number of victims?

Let's examine that idea for a moment.

According to Wikipedia.com, the 12 most prolific serial killers in American history (with victim numbers in parenthesis) are; Gary Ridgeway (49); Donald Harvey (37); Theodore Robert Bundy (35); John Wayne Gacy (33); Jane Toppan (31); Dean Corll (28); Juan Corona (25); Wayne Williams (24); Ronald Dominique (23); Earle Nelson (22); Patrick Kearney (21); and William Bonin (21).

A horrible collective, I'm sure you'll agree. But a quick glance at the list tells me that I've included only five of these cases on my "Worst of" list.

Why is that?

Well, first off, victim numbers are not as reliable as they at first seem. Generally, these figures are derived from murders for which the killer has been convicted. But it is not uncommon for jurisdictions to opt out of putting a serial killer on trial for a particular murder. This may apply if the killer has already been convicted elsewhere, or if the prosecution does not believe they have a winnable case.

Then there's the issue of confessions. Serial killers (and psychopaths in general) are habitual liars. Often, as in the cases of Henry Lee Lucas and Donald Leroy Evans, they claim credit for crimes they didn't commit. In other instances, they'll withhold information for use as a bargaining tool, or as a means of taunting the authorities or the victims' families. As a result, published victim numbers tend to be unreliable.

And are victim numbers the best criteria for ranking such a list anyway? What about level of depravity? What about degree of infamy?

Yes, I know these criteria are nebulous, but should they not play a part? If the intention is to compile a list of the "worst" serial killers, then I believe they must, since relying solely on victim count would exclude such infamous psychos as David Berkowitz and Jeffrey Dahmer.

In the end, a list such as the one presented in this book, comes down to the author's own particular bias, the cases that fascinate or frighten him. That is certainly the filter I've applied, selecting cases based on a loose conglomeration of ranking factors, including the aforementioned, victim count, level of depravity, and degree of infamy. I've also added another metric. Call it the "fear factor," call it the "degree of creepiness," the ability of a case to get under one's skin.

The decision to cap the list at 12 also means that a number of notorious cases have been omitted. Those that almost made the cut, but didn't, include the Hillside Strangler, Earle Nelson, Wayne Williams and Coral Watts. Perhaps they might form the basis for another book.

Here then are the 12 deadly psychopaths I consider to be the worst serial killers in American criminal history.

David Berkowitz

Son of Sam

"Hello from the cracks in the sidewalks of New York City and from the ants that dwell in those cracks and feed on the dried blood of the dead..." David Berkowitz a.k.a. Son of Sam

For a period of just over a year, from the summer of 1976 until August 1977, the city of New York was terrorized by a brutal and murderous gunman. The killer emerged like a phantom out of the night, his heavy caliber weapon shattering the dark as he fired at couples sitting in parked cars, or women walking alone. By the time he was done, six young lives would be snuffed out, many others shattered. And the world would know a fearsome new name, "Son of Sam."

The first shooting occurred in the Pelham Bay area of the Bronx. Just after one o'clock on the morning of July 29, 1976, 18-year-old Donna Lauria and her friend Jody Valenti were sitting in Donna's

Oldsmobile. The girls had just returned from a local disco and were discussing their evening when Donna's father stopped by the car and told her it was time to come inside. Donna said that she'd come up soon, but as she opened the door, she noticed a man quickly approaching the vehicle, a paper bag in his hand. "What is this?" she said, but she'd hardly spoken the words when the man suddenly produced a pistol from the bag. He dropped into a shooter's stance with one elbow braced on his knee and the weapon held in both hands. Then he fired - his first shot hitting Donna in the head and killing her instantly, his second striking Jody in the thigh. Three more shots were fired before the killer turned and walked quickly away.

Despite her injury, Jody scrambled from the car and screamed for help. Donna's father heard the commotion and came running out of the apartment. In his pajamas and bare feet, he raced the car to the hospital, hoping to save his daughter's life. It was too late.

Three months after the senseless murder of Donna Lauria, 20-year-old Carl Denaro was attending a going away party at a bar in Queens. In a few days, he'd be joining the Air Force and he was enjoying his last days of civilian life by hanging out with his buddies. Also attending the get-together was Rosemary Keenan, a friend of Carl's from college.

After the party broke up at around 2:30, Carl drove with Rosemary back to Forest Hills Gardens, stopping outside her apartment to talk for a while. As they sat in the car, a man suddenly appeared beside the passenger window. He drew a gun and fired five times, hitting Carl in the head. Unhurt but terrified, Rosemary started the car and raced off, eventually bringing Carl to the hospital. He would survive the attack but would need a metal plate in his head to repair his shattered skull.

The Denaro/Keenan shooting bore startling similarities to the Lauria/Valenti case, but because the crimes had occurred in different boroughs and were therefore investigated by different precincts, police did not yet see a pattern. That would change.

Shortly after midnight, on the evening of November 26, 1976, 16-year-old Donna DeMasi and her 18-year-old friend, Joanne Lomino, were talking on Joanne's porch, having just come home from a late night movie. As they spoke, a young man dressed in military fatigues approached them. "Do you know where...?" he started, as though about to ask for directions. He never finished the question. Instead, he reached into his jacket and produced a gun, then fired two shots, hitting both girls. He then fired three more shots at the house before walking quickly away.

The sound of gunfire and the girls' screams brought the Lomino family running from the house where they found Joanne and Donna, gravely injured. They were rushed to hospital where surgeons fought to save them. Both girls survived. In Donna's case, the bullet had passed right through her body, coming within a quarter inch of her spine. Joanne was not so lucky, the bullet shattered several vertebrae, rendering her a paraplegic.

There were no further attacks through the holiday season and into the new year. Then, during the early hours of January 30, 1977, the killer struck again.

Twenty-six-year-old Christine Freund and her fiancé John Diel had just been to a movie and were sitting in Diel's car trying to decide what to do with the rest of their evening. At around 12:40 a.m. a man approached the passenger side of the vehicle and fired three shots. Diel drove off in panic, then headed for the nearest hospital when he saw that Christine had been hit. She'd suffered two bullet wounds to the head and died several hours later. Diel suffered only superficial injuries. He hadn't seen the man who had fired at them.

The murder of Christine Freund was assigned to NYPD Detective Sergeant Joe Coffey. Coffey, an experienced homicide investigator, feared that the murder may have been perpetrated by a psycho with a grudge against women. Following this line of inquiry, he soon came across the details of the other shootings. Coffey then took his findings to his captain, Joe Borelli.

A look at the ballistics proved that Coffey might be onto something. All of the bullets had been fired from a .44, and from a very unusual weapon at that, a Charter Arms Bulldog. With the realization that a serial shooter might be prowling the streets of New York, a task force was formed under Captain Borelli. The first public admission that the shootings might be related soon followed. But the killer wasn't done yet, and for the next murder, he varied his M.O.

At around 7:30 p.m. on March 8, 1977, 19-year-old Columbia University student, Virginia Voskerichian, was walking home from school. As she followed Dartmouth Street (just a block from where Christine Freund had been shot), a man approached, walking directly towards her. As the distance closed, he suddenly produced a gun. Virginia raised her textbooks in front of her face in a desperate and futile attempt to save herself. The bullet passed right through and struck her in the face, killing her instantly.

As the killer fled the scene, he offered a chirpy, "Hi, mister," to a middle-aged man who had witnessed the murder. A passing patrol car also spotted a running man. But when they heard on their radio that a woman had been shot, they raced to the scene to see if they could offer assistance.

Captain Joe Borelli (quoted by Laurence D. Klausner in his book on the case) best sums up the feelings of the NYPD at this point. "If you watch detectives at any homicide, you'll notice that they go about their jobs unemotionally... they didn't want to look at her. They knew it was senseless. She was someone beautiful and she was lying under the sheet, a bullet in her face had destroyed her. It began to grab at them, in the guts, and they just turned away. These were veterans and they couldn't take it."

The police were frustrated and felt powerless to catch the killer, but at least they had a ballistics match and an eyewitness description of the man they were looking for. The .44 Caliber Killer (as the press were now calling him), was "a white male, 25 to 30 years of age, six feet tall, of medium build, and with dark hair."

In the wake of the latest killings, the city of New York put more resources behind catching the killer. Deputy Inspector Timothy Dowd was appointed to head up a team of more than 300 officers dedicated to the task. It seemed the .44 Caliber Killer couldn't possibly commit another murder without being caught. But he did.

On April 17, 1977, a young couple were making out in their parked car near the Hutchinson River Parkway. Valentina Suriani was 18, an aspiring actress and model. Her boyfriend, 20-year-old Alexander Esau, was a tow truck operator. At around 3 a.m. on that Sunday morning, a car pulled up beside them, its driver leaning out and firing four shots, hitting each of them twice. Valentina died at the scene, Alexander a while later in the hospital.

But this time, there was something different. The killer had left behind a letter.

David Berkowitz would later admit that reading a book about Jack the Ripper had given him the idea of sending letters to the police and media. This first letter was a rambling, handwritten missive addressed to NYPD Captain Joseph Borelli. It expressed the killer's intention of continuing his "work" and taunted the police for their failure to catch him. But the most significant revelation in the letter was the name the killer gave himself, "I am the Son of Sam," he wrote, and although the contents of the letter were withheld from the public, some of it leaked to the press. Soon after, the ".44 Caliber Killer" moniker was gone. New York's elusive serial killer was now the "Son of Sam."

The next letter was addressed to Jimmy Breslin, a reporter for the Daily News. "Hello from the cracks in the sidewalks of NYC," Berkowitz wrote, "and from the ants that dwell in these cracks and feed on the dried blood of the dead that has settled into the cracks."

The letter also went on to make the veiled threat: "Don't think because you haven't heard from me for a while that I went to sleep. No, rather, I am still here. Like a spirit roaming the night. Thirsty, hungry, seldom stopping to rest; anxious to please Sam. Sam's a thirsty lad. He won't let me stop killing until he gets his fill of blood. Tell me, Jim, what will you have for July 29?"

Although the Daily News withheld portions of the letter (at the insistence of police), the reference to July 29 sparked panic in the city. July 29 would be the anniversary of the first shooting, the murder of Donna Lauria. Because all of the female victims thus far had had long, dark hair, hair salons were suddenly overwhelmed with requests for cuts and dye jobs. There was also a run on wigs, with many suppliers selling out.

But the killer didn't wait until July 29. He reappeared on June 26, shooting Sal Lupo, 20, and Judy Placido, 17, soon after they left the Elephas discotheque in the Bayside area of Queens. The young couple had been sitting in their car at about 3:00 a.m. when three gunshots were fired at them. Both were hit but suffered only minor injuries. Neither had seen their attacker.

As the one-year anniversary of the first murder approached, police put a massive force of uniformed and plain-clothes officers on the street, focusing their efforts mainly on the killer's usual hunting grounds of the Bronx and Queens.

But the night passed without incident. When the Son of Sam reappeared two nights later, it was in Brooklyn.

At about 2:30 on the morning of July 31, 1977, Stacy Moskowitz
and Robert Violante, both 20, were sitting in Violante's car,
stopped under a streetlight near a park in the neighborhood of
Bath Beach. While they sat kissing, a man approached and fired
four shots, hitting both of them in the head before running off.

The police were soon on the scene and rushed the victims to
Coney Island Hospital from where they were airlifted to Kings
County Hospital, which had more advanced facilities for dealing
with head trauma. Despite the desperate efforts of surgeons to
save her life, Stacy Moskowitz died hours later. Bobby Violante
survived, but lost his left eye and had only 20 percent vision in his
right.

This time, though, there'd been a number of witnesses to the crime
and one of them, Cecelia Davis, would provide police with a vital
clue. Around the time of the Moskowitz/Violante shooting, Davis
had been walking her dog when she saw a parked car being
ticketed. Moments later, a young man walked from the direction of
the car and passed her by. She noticed something in his hand, a
"dark object" as she described it. The way the man looked at her
made her afraid. She hurried home, but a moment later heard
shots fired from behind her. Davis had been terrified and had
waited four days before coming forward. Now, though, the police
had a lead. They checked out all vehicles ticketed in the area that
night. One of them was a 1970 Ford Galaxy owned by David
Berkowitz.

The NYPD would later state that they immediately considered
Berkowitz the main suspect, but that is unlikely. Most probably
they wanted to question him as a potential witness when they

contacted the Yonkers police on August 9 and asked them to schedule an interview with Berkowitz.

Yonkers PD had, in fact, already identified Berkowitz as a potential 'Son of Sam' suspect. They believed him to be the person behind a number of unusual crimes committed in their jurisdiction and thought he may have alluded to some of those crimes in the Son of Sam letters.

The following day, August 10, 1977, police arrived outside Berkowitz's apartment in Pine Street, Yonkers. Berkowitz's yellow Ford Galaxy stood at the curb and officers noticed a rifle lying on the backseat. Inside the car, they found a duffel bag filled with ammunition, maps of the crime scenes, and a threatening letter addressed to Det. Sgt. Dowd of the Omega task force.

Believing now that they had their man, officers decided to wait Berkowitz out, rather than go up to his apartment. In the meantime, they requested a warrant for the vehicle. The warrant hadn't arrived yet when Berkowitz stepped from his apartment building onto the sidewalk. He walked towards his car carrying a paper bag. Detectives let him get into the vehicle before they moved in. The bag he was carrying contained his .44 Charter Arms Bulldog.

"Well, you got me. How come it took you such a long time?" Berkowitz said.

"Who have I got?" the arresting officer asked.

"You know," Berkowitz said coyly.

"No, I don't. You tell me."

"I'm Sam. David Berkowitz."

After his arrest, Berkowitz was held briefly in Yonkers before being transported to Police Headquarters in New York City where his interrogation began on August 11, 1977. After just 30 minutes of questioning, he confessed to all of the murders. He said that a demon in the form of his neighbor's dog had instructed him to kill, demanding the blood of pretty young girls. The "Sam" mentioned in the letters was the dog's owner, Sam Carr, who Berkowitz said was also a powerful demon.

On June 12, 1978, David Berkowitz was sentenced to 25 years to life for each of the murders, to be served consecutively. During sentencing, Berkowitz repeatedly chanted, in a voice just loud enough to hear, "Stacy was a whore"(referencing his last victim, Stacy Moskowitz). This behavior caused an uproar among Moskowitz's relatives present in the courtroom and the trial eventually had to be adjourned to restore order.

Berkowitz began serving his sentence at Sing Sing before transfer to the Clinton Correctional Facility and then to Attica, where he spent more than a decade. He is currently incarcerated at the Sullivan Correctional Facility in Fallsburg, New York.

At a press conference in February 1979, he admitted that his claims of demonic possession were a hoax. His real motive for the murders was anger over his lack of success with women, which was why he specifically targeted attractive young females as his victims.

William Bonin

The Freeway Killer

"I couldn't stop killing. It got easier each time." William Bonin

During the late seventies and early eighties, a trio of deadly serial killers prowled the highways and bi-ways of Southern California, leaving a trail of mutilated bodies in their wake. One of these men was a necrophile, dispatching his victims swiftly with a bullet to the head before carrying out his sickening perversions on their corpses. The other two were sadists, keeping their victims alive for as long as possible while they inflicted the most inhumane tortures on them. Between them, Patrick Kearney, Randy Kraft, and William Bonin were responsible for at least 113 deaths.

William Bonin did not have the best start in life. Born in January 1947, to parents who were both alcoholics, the boy and his two brothers suffered severe neglect and abuse. His father was a compulsive gambler who once lost the family home to his gambling debts, and William's bingo-obsessed mother often left her children unfed, filthy and unclothed, their wellbeing reliant on the charity of neighbors. When she tired of even these meager attempts at parenting, she passed the boys off on their grandfather, a convicted pedophile.

It was no surprise, then, that the youngster got into trouble with the law. In 1957, aged just 10, William was arrested for stealing license plates and sent to a reformatory. Here he suffered yet more abuse. Beatings and inhumane punishments (like submersion in freezing water) were common, as were knifepoint rapes by other inmates. By his teens he was back in the dubious care of his mother and had become an abuser himself, preying on neighborhood children and even his own brother.

Bonin graduated high school in 1965 and shortly thereafter joined the U.S. Air Force. He served in Vietnam where he logged 700 hours as an aerial gunner and was awarded a Good Conduct medal. It was only after his honorable discharge, in October 1968, that the military became aware that Bonin had sexually assaulted two fellow soldiers at gunpoint.

Back in the States, he lived for a short while with his mother in Connecticut before moving to California where he soon alerted the attention of the authorities. In 1969, he was arrested for kidnapping and sexually assaulting five youths, aged between 12 and 18, in Los Angeles County. In each of these cases, Bonin picked up the boys in his van, handcuffed them and then forced them to perform oral sex before he sodomized them.

Bonin pled guilty, but rather than receiving jail time, he was sent to Atascadero State Hospital where he was examined by a procession of neurologists, psychiatrists and psychologists. They found a number of worrying signs, both physical and psychological; suspected damage to the frontal lobe; signs of manic-depression; and several unexplained scars on his head.

Despite this, Bonin secured his release in May 1974, after doctors declared him, "no longer a danger to others."

Within 16 months, he was in trouble again, this time for the gunpoint rape of a 14-year-old hitchhiker named David McVicker. It earned him 1 to 15 years at the California Men's Facility in San Luis Obispo.

Released in October 1978, Bonin moved to an apartment complex in Downey, southeast Los Angeles County, where he found employment as a truck driver. Soon after, he became acquainted with a 43-year-old neighbor named Everett Fraser and started attending the frequent parties that Fraser threw. It was at one of these parties that Bonin first met 22-year-old Vernon Butts and 19-year-old Gregory Miley, soon to be his accomplices in a horrific murder spree.

Yet, for now, Bonin was still managing to restrain his murderous urges. Less than a year after his release for the McVicker attack, he found himself in custody again, after sexually assaulting a 17-year-old hitchhiker. Bonin was still on probation at this time, and the crime should have sent him back to prison to complete a 15-year stretch. However, an administrative mix-up allowed him to walk free.

Everett Fraser picked Bonin up from the Orange County Jail. He'd later recall that on the drive home, Bonin told him: "No one's going to testify again. This is never going to happen to me again."

Shortly after this conversation, the series of murders by the fiend who the media dubbed "The Freeway Killer," began.

The first murder attributed to Bonin was carried out with the aid of his accomplice Vernon Butts, a low-life drifter with a lengthy rap sheet. On the morning of May 28, 1979, 13-year-old Thomas Glen Lundgren left his parents' home in Reseda in order to visit a friend. The boy was hitchhiking when Bonin and Butts picked him up. His mutilated corpse was found the next day in Agoura. He'd been emasculated, and an autopsy would reveal that he'd been slashed, stabbed, and bludgeoned before being strangled to death.

Two months later, on August 4, 1979, Bonin and Butts abducted 17-year-old Mark Shelton as he walked to a movie theater near Beach Boulevard, Westminster. Shelton was sodomized with foreign objects, which caused his body to go into shock that proved fatal. His corpse was discarded alongside a freeway in San Bernardino County.

Perhaps disappointed with the premature death of their last victim, Bonin and Butts took another teenager the following day. Seventeen-year-old German student, Markus Grabs, was hitchhiking the Pacific Coast Highway when Bonin and Butts offered him a ride. He was bound and taken to Bonin's home where he was sodomized, beaten and stabbed over 70 times. His nude body was discarded in Malibu Canyon.

The unholy duo waited three weeks before striking again. On August 27, the mutilated corpse of 15-year-old Donald Hyden was discovered in a dumpster near the Ventura Freeway. He had last been seen in Santa Monica the previous day. Hyden had been raped and strangled and his throat had been cut. An attempt had also been made to castrate him.

On September 9, 1979, Bonin and Butts encountered 17-year-old David Murillo cycling to a movie theater. They lured Murillo into Bonin's van where he was bound, raped, bludgeoned and strangled before his body was discarded alongside Highway 101. Eight days later, they abducted 18-year-old Robert Wirostek as he cycled to work. His ravaged body was discovered on September 19, beside Interstate 10.

Despite the similarities in these crimes, Orange and Los Angeles County officials continued to deny that they had a serial killer in their midst. And they may have felt vindicated in this belief, as nearly three months passed without another murder. However, by the end of November, the Freeway Killer was back, taking three victims in under a fortnight.

The first victim was an unidentified youth whose savagely beaten body was discovered in Kern County. The following day, Bonin abducted and strangled 17-year-old Frank Fox, leaving his body on a stretch of highway five miles east of San Diego. Ten days later, he murdered a 15-year-old Long Beach youth named John Kilpatrick. Kilpatrick was last seen leaving his parents' home to meet up with some friends. His body was found beside a road in a remote area of Rialto.

And on New Year's Day, 1980, Bonin brutalized and strangled a 16-year-old Rialto youth named Michael Francis McDonald, dumping his body in San Bernardino County, where it was found two days later.

In the last few murders, Bonin had acted alone. On February 3, 1980, he brought in a new accomplice, another sexual psychopath, named Gregory Matthew Miley. The pair picked up 15-year-old Charles Miranda in West Hollywood then drove him to an isolated spot where Bonin sodomized him. When Miley was unable to sustain an erection to do the same, he became frustrated and raped the teen with a blunt object. Bonin then strangled Miranda using the boy's shirt and a tire iron to form a tourniquet. They dumped the body in an alley, but Bonin immediately announced, "I'm still horny. Let's do another one."

A few hours later, they found 12-year-old James McCabe waiting at a stop for a bus to Disneyland. The boy accepted a ride, but as Miley drove, Bonin forced McCabe into the back where he beat and raped him. Later Bonin strangled the boy by forcing a tire iron down on his throat while Miley jumped repeatedly on the child's chest. James McCabe's naked, battered body was found three days later, alongside a dumpster in the city of Walnut. Miley later said that he and Bonin used the $6 found in the boy's wallet to buy lunch.

There was no stopping Bonin now. He was obsessed with murder, addicted to it. He would later tell a court-appointed psychiatrist that he became excited at the prospect of killing someone. He could barely wait for sundown so he could go cruising to pick up his next victim.

A rapid spree of murders followed. Ronald Gatlin, 18, disappeared from North Hollywood on March 14, 1980. His body was discovered the next day in Duarte, beaten strangled and stabbed with an ice pick. Harry Todd Turner, 14, disappeared from Hollywood on March 20. He was discovered five days later near the Santa Monica Freeway, his body marked with bites and cigarette burns (Bonin was assisted in this murder by an accomplice named William Pugh). Glen Norman Barker, 14, of Huntington Beach, was sexually assaulted and strangled, his body found March 22, beside the Ortega Highway with another body in close proximity, that of 15-year-old Russell Duane Rugh, who had disappeared while waiting for a bus to work.

And still, the killings continued. Steven Wood, 16, went missing on his way to school on April 10, 1980. His body was found the next day. The same day, Lawrence Eugene Sharp, 18, of Long Beach, disappeared. His body showed up on May 18, in a trash bin behind a Westminster service station.

On April 29, Bonin and Butts abducted Darin Lee Kendrick, 19, from a Stanton store where he worked. In a particularly brutal murder, even by their standards, Kendrick was forced to swallow hydrochloric acid and an ice pick was forced through his ear causing a fatal wound to the upper cervical spinal cord. His body was found the next morning.

On May 19, Bonin asked Butts to go out with him on another killing. When Butts declined, he went out alone and abducted 14-year-old Sean King from a bus stop in Downey. The boy's raped and strangled body was discarded in Yucaipa.

Not long after this latest murder, Bonin invited a 19-year-old, homeless drifter by the name of James Munro to stay with him. Soon he'd persuaded Munro to accompany him on his next murder run. Unbeknownst to Bonin, his rampage was about to come to an abrupt end.

On May 29, 1980, William Pugh, who had assisted Bonin in the murder of Harry Todd Turner, was picked up on an auto theft charge. Once in custody, Pugh confided to a counselor that he believed William Bonin to be the "Freeway Killer." The counselor passed this information on to LAPD homicide detective John St. John who did a background check on Bonin and picked up his string of convictions for sexually assaulting teenage boys. St. John then arranged for Bonin to be put under surveillance, which began on June 2.

Unfortunately, the surveillance began too late to save Bonin's next victim. On the morning of June 2, 1980, Bonin and James Munro picked up 19-year-old Steven Wells. They lured the youth back to Bonin's apartment and after Bonin and Wells had sex, Bonin offered $200 if Wells would allow himself to be tied up. Wells agreed, but as soon as he was bound, Bonin began assaulting him. According to Munro he went into another room and watched TV, although Bonin disputes this and says Munro participated in the murder.

Once Wells was dead, Bonin and Munro loaded his body into the van and drove to Vernon Butts' apartment. Bonin asked for Butts' advice in disposing of the body and was told, "Try a gas station - like where we dumped the last one."

By June 11, Bonin had been under surveillance for nine days, with no sign of criminality on his part. However, on that day, Bonin went cruising again. The surveillance team watched him try to pick up five separate teenagers before he succeeded in luring a youth into his van. The police followed him as he drove to a deserted parking lot. By the time they approached the van and threw the doors open, Bonin had the boy bound and was in the process of sodomizing him. The Freeway Killer was caught at last.

Once in custody, Bonin confessed to 21 murders, naming Vernon Butts as his primary accomplice and describing each crime in horrifying detail. Butts was arrested on July 25, and the arrests of James Munro and Gregory Miley followed soon after. Police also learned that William Pugh, who'd led them to Bonin, was far from innocent himself, and had participated in the murder of Harry Todd Turner.

Bonin's trial began on November 5, 1981, and lasted until January 5, 1982. The jury deliberated for six days before delivering a guilty verdict in 10 of the murders and recommending the death penalty.

However, it would be 14 years before that sentence was eventually carried out. On February 23, 1996, William Bonin became the first person to be executed by lethal injection in the state of California.

Of Bonin's accomplices, Vernon Butts committed suicide in custody three months after his arrest. Miley, Munro and Pugh all agreed to testify against Bonin to avoid the death penalty. Miley and Munro received life terms. Pugh got six years on a reduced charge of manslaughter.

The Boston Strangler

It is one of the most infamous serial killer cases in U.S history, the first case extensively covered by mass-market television, radio and the national press, a case that sparked widespread panic in the city of Boston, a case that continues to fascinate, even to this day.

Between June 1962 and January 1964, 13 Massachusetts women fell victim to a serial killer, a fiend who has gone down in history by the notorious epithet, the Boston Strangler. The killer entered the homes of his victims without force, apparently talking his way in. Once inside, he sexually molested the women before strangling them with articles of clothing and fleeing the scene. Many of the victims were posed, others had sexually degrading post-mortem acts performed upon them, all were killed in their own homes.

Albert De Salvo, a hyper-sexed factory worker, sex offender and petty criminal, confessed to the crimes, and although he was never officially charged with the murders, he entered the public consciousness as the Strangler, a belief that held for decades. Yet there is significant evidence to suggest that De Salvo was not the killer. Indeed, many of the detectives working the case believed that the murders were not the work of a single man but of two, and possibly more, perpetrators, working independently.

The first murder occurred on June 14, 1962. Anna Slesers, a 55-year-old divorcee living in the Back Bay area was due to attend a memorial service that evening and had arranged for her son, Juris, to pick her up at 7 o'clock. However, when Juris arrived at his mother's apartment, there was no reply.

At first, Juris was annoyed, then concerned, when his pounding on the door brought no response. Eventually, he applied his shoulder to the door and forced it open. His worst fears were confirmed as he walked through the apartment and saw his mother lying on the bathroom floor with the cord from her robe wound tightly around her neck.

Responding to the call, detectives James Mellon and John Driscoll found the petite woman provocatively displayed, the cloth cord of her housecoat knotted around her neck, and tied in a decorative bow. The apartment appeared to have been ransacked, although a gold watch and several pieces of jewelry, left out in the open, had not been taken.

Just a couple of weeks later, on June 30, there was another murder. Nina Nichols lived alone in an apartment in the Brighton area of Boston. The 68-year-old, retired physiotherapist was found sexually assaulted and strangled with a pair of nylon stockings, the ends knotted in a bow. As with the Slesers murder, Nina Nichols' body had been posed and the apartment ransacked, although none of her valuables had been taken.

That same day, in the suburb of Lynn, some 15 miles north of Boston, an almost identical murder was committed. Helen Blake, a 65-year-old divorcee, was raped, and then strangled with a stocking, her body left suggestively posed. Her apartment had been thoroughly ransacked, but although two diamond rings were missing, other valuables were left untouched.

This latest murder set alarm bells jangling at police headquarters. Three homicides in a relatively small area, over a period of just two weeks, all of them bearing a clear signature, and quite possibly committed by the same man. As Police Commissioner Edmund McNamara canceled all police leave and put detectives on the ground checking on known sex offenders, a warning went out via the media to Boston's women. They were advised to keep doors locked and to be wary of admitting strangers to their homes.

These measures didn't deter the Strangler at all. On August 21, 75-year-old, Ida Irga, was found dead in her apartment. The shy, retiring widow had been strangled with a pillowcase, her nude body posed flat on its back, each ankle resting on a chair, the placement (facing the door) designed for maximum shock value. She'd been dead two days by the time she was found.

Just 24 hours later, came another grisly discovery. Jane Sullivan, a 67-year-old nurse, lived across town from Ida Irga, in Dorchester. She had been dead for 10 days before her body was found, laid out in her bathtub. The condition of the corpse made it impossible to determine whether she'd been sexually assaulted or not.

As panic gripped the city of Boston, there was a three-month reprieve before the next murder. This crime, however, was somewhat different. Up until now, the Strangler had targeted older victims, but Sophie Clark, an attractive, African-American student, was just 21-years-old. On December 5, 1962, Sophie's roommates returned home to find her nude body, lying legs apart, three nylon stockings knotted tightly around her neck. She'd been sexually assaulted and there was semen found on the rug close to her body.

There was no sign of forced entry which Sophie's roommates thought was strange. They assured the detectives that Sophie had been extremely security conscious, insisting on an extra lock on the door and even questioning friends before admitting them to the apartment.

As police questioned the neighbors, an interesting lead turned up. Mrs. Marcella Lulka told officers that around 2:20 that afternoon a man had knocked on her door and said that the building manager had sent him to speak to her about painting her apartment. He'd then complimented her on her figure, and asked if she'd ever thought of modeling.

Mrs. Lulka had asked the man to be quiet, by raising a finger to her lips. She'd told him that her husband was asleep in the next room and he'd then said it was the wrong apartment and hurried away. The man was 25 to 30 years old, she said, of average height with honey-colored hair. He'd been wearing a dark jacket and dark green trousers.

A check with the building manager revealed that he hadn't engaged anyone to do any painting, leading police to suspect that this man was the Strangler, especially as Sophie Clark was killed at around 2:30 in the afternoon. Why, though, had the security conscious Sophie let him in?

Three weeks after the murder of Sophie Clark, a 23-year-old secretary named Patricia Bissette failed to show up for work. Her boss was concerned about her, so he called on her apartment. Getting no response when he knocked, he tracked down the building superintendent and the two of them entered the apartment through a window.

They found Patricia Bissette lying face up in bed, the covers drawn up to her chin. Several stockings were knotted around her neck. The medical examiner would later confirm that she'd been raped and possibly sodomized.

On Wednesday, May 8, 1963, friends of Beverly Samans, a 23-year-old graduate student, became concerned when she didn't show up for choir practice at the Second Unitarian Church in Back Bay. A friend went to her apartment to check on Beverley, entering with a key that she had given him. As the man opened the front door, a shocking scene awaited him. Beverley's nude body lay in plain view, her legs splayed, a nylon stocking and two handkerchiefs woven together and knotted around her neck. The cause of death wasn't strangulation, though, she'd been stabbed 22 times.

The summer of 1963 brought another break in the killings. Then, on September 8, 1963, a 58-year-old divorcee, named Evelyn Corbin, was found strangled in her home in Salem, Massachusetts. Two nylon stockings were knotted around her neck and her panties were stuffed into her mouth as a gag. Her apartment had been ransacked but valuables lying in plain sight hadn't been taken.

On November 25, while Bostonians joined the rest of the country in grieving the death of assassinated President John F. Kennedy, another murder occurred. Joann Graff was a 23-year-old industrial designer. She'd been dead three days by the time her body was found with two nylon stockings tied in an elaborate bow around her neck. There were teeth marks on her breast and there was evidence that she'd been sexually assaulted.

As detectives questioned other residents in the building, they uncovered a clue that provided a link to the Sophie Clark case. A student who lived in the apartment above Joann reported that, at around 3:25 p.m. on the day of the murder, a stranger had knocked on his door. The man was about mid-twenties with elaborately pomaded hair, dressed in dark green slacks and a dark shirt and jacket. The man asked if Joann Graff lived there (pronouncing her name incorrectly as "Joan"). The student had said no and directed the man to the correct apartment. A moment later he heard knocking from the floor below and then a door opening and closing. When a friend of Joann's phoned her 10 minutes later, there was no reply.

Just over a month later on January 4, 1964, two young women returned home to a gruesome discovery. Their roommate, 19-year-old Mary Sullivan, lay murdered, displayed in a shocking fashion. She was posed, sitting upright on a bed. Two stockings and a pink silk scarf were knotted around her neck, and a "Happy New Year" card rested against her feet. A thick liquid that looked like semen was dripping from her mouth onto her breasts. A broomstick handle had been rammed into her vagina.

The brutal murder of Mary Sullivan and the disrespectful way in which she had been posed was the last straw for Massachusetts Attorney General Edward Brooke. On January 17, 1964, he announced that he was personally taking charge of the case. In short order, Brooke ordered the formation of a task force, formally called the Special Division of Crime Research and Detection. He

placed Assistant Attorney General John S. Bottomly in charge of
the team, a controversial choice as Bottomly had no experience of
criminal law and was universally disliked by the senior hierarchy
of the Boston Police Department.

And Bottomly's first action hardly improved his standing with his
police colleagues. He brought in Peter Hurkos, a controversial
Dutch psychic who seemed to make a habit of involving himself in
high-profile murder investigations. Hurkos had achieved some
limited measure of success in the past, most notably in the Melvin
Rees case, but he failed woefully in identifying the Boston
Strangler. The suspect he named could be categorically cleared of
involvement in any of the murders. It was a blow to Hurkos'
credibility and to that of the task force.

At this point in the story, it is necessary to make a small detour, to
a bizarre series of sex offenses that occurred in the Cambridge
area a couple of years before the Boston Strangler appeared on the
scene. Over a period of three months, a man in his late twenties
took to knocking on doors and introducing himself as the
representative of a modeling agency. He'd tell any woman who
answered that she'd been recommended to the agency, and ask if
he could measure her to ascertain that she met the agency's
requirements. Many of women, flattered by the attention and
interested in the money he said they could earn, allowed him to
take their measurements. That done, he'd thank them, and say he'd
be in touch. Of course, they never heard from him again and most
of the women put it down as a harmless prank. Others, though,
were offended and reported the matter to the police.

On March 17, 1961, Cambridge police apprehended a man trying
to break into a house. Under questioning, the man confessed to
being the "Measuring Man." He was Albert De Salvo, a 29-year-old

Bostonian with numerous arrests for breaking and entering. Asked what the point of his "Measuring Man" charade was, he said it was a prank to get one over smart, high-class people. Prank or not, De Salvo's got 18 months. He was released in April 1962, two months before the first Boston Strangler murder.

In November of 1964, almost three years after his release from prison, and 11 months after the murder of Mary Sullivan, De Salvo was arrested again. This time, the charges were more serious. On October 27, he had entered a residence and placed a knife to a woman's throat as she dozed. He tied her up and stuffed underwear in her mouth then stripped her naked and fondled her before fleeing the apartment. Before he left he apologized for what he'd done.

The woman had gotten a good look at her attacker and her description reminded the investigating officers of the Measuring Man. They brought De Salvo in, and the victim identified him from a lineup. A check with other jurisdictions turned up an interest from Connecticut. They'd had a number of similar attacks there and had given their unknown assailant the nickname, "The Green Man," because he always wore green work pants.

Faced with the accusations, De Salvo admitted to breaking into over 400 apartments and assaulting over 300 women. The police took these numbers with a pinch of salt. De Salvo was well known as a braggart with a habit of exaggerating. Nonetheless, he was in serious trouble.

De Salvo was sent to Bridgewater State Hospital for observation where his cellmate was a man named George Nassar, accused of the execution-style killing of a gas station attendant. Although he was a vicious killer, who'd previously served time for another murder, Nasser was an intelligent man. He possessed a near-genius IQ and spoke several languages. He was also known for his ability to manipulate, and at Bridgewater, he became Albert De Salvo's confidant. Not long after, Nasser placed a call to his attorney, F. Lee Bailey and Bailey took a flight from the west coast to meet with De Salvo.

No one knows why Albert De Salvo confessed to being the Boston Strangler. It has been speculated that he and Nasser cooked up a scheme whereby De Salvo would confess and Nasser would turn him in and claim the reward money, which they'd later split. De Salvo expected to go to prison for life anyway, the money would go to his wife and two kids. Another theory is that the smooth talking Nasser convinced De Salvo that there was a fortune to be made in book and movie rights. And it should also not be discounted that De Salvo was a braggart and a blowhard. The idea of being recognized as the infamous Boston Strangler must have appealed to him.

Whatever the motivation, F. Lee Bailey interviewed De Salvo at Bridgewater and then set up a meeting with Lieutenants Donovan and Sherry of the Strangler Task Force. At that meeting, he played them a tape of his interview with De Salvo, containing a confession to the Strangler murders. To the hard-pressed detectives of the Strangler task force, under increasing public and official scrutiny, De Salvo's confession must have been like manna from heaven. And there was no chance that it could be a fake. De Salvo's knowledge of the crime scenes was far too detailed, containing information that only the killer would know.

A meeting was hastily arranged between Police Commissioner McNamara, Dr. Ames Robey, the psychiatrist at Bridgewater, and De Salvo. This interview began on September 29, 1965, and resulted in more than 50 hours of tape and over 2000 pages of transcript. Again, De Salvo's detailed recollection of the crimes was impressive. Now, the police were faced with the arduous task of checking the details to make sure that De Salvo was telling the truth.

While they were doing that, De Salvo's attorney, F. Lee Bailey, sat down with Attorney General Brooke and John Bottomly, to thrash out a deal. Bailey came straight to the point. Despite De Salvo's confession, he did not believe that the State of Massachusetts had enough evidence to successfully try him as the Boston Strangler. However, De Salvo was prepared to plead guilty to the Green Man assaults, and to accept a life sentence for those crimes.

Brook and Bottomly considered their options and decided that Bailey was right. Putting De Salvo on trial constituted a huge risk, as the court proceedings would fall right in the middle of Brook's election campaign for the senate. A loss in court would seriously dent his chances. He thus agreed to Bailey's terms.

De Salvo went on trial on for the Green Man charges on January 10, 1967, and was sentenced to life in prison. However, he would serve less than seven years of his sentence.

In November 1973, while in the infirmary at Walpole State Prison, Albert De Salvo was stabbed to death by an unknown assailant. The day before his death he had placed a call to Dr. Ames Robey. De Salvo was frantic, saying he had information to share on the Boston Strangler case and that he feared for his life. Dr. Robey agreed to meet with him the next morning, but De Salvo was murdered that night. His killer has never been caught.

So was Albert De Salvo the Boston Strangler? The evidence suggests that he was not. But if that is the case, it begs the question, how could he have had such intimate knowledge of the crime scenes?

The truth is that De Salvo got as much information wrong as he got right and that most of the so-called "intimate detail" he offered was public knowledge, having been reported in the papers. It is true that he did provide some details that had been withheld from the public. But that information might easily have been fed to him, either by the real killer or by members of the Strangler task force, desperate to close the case.

Yet, even if we assume that De Salvo gained most of his knowledge by following the case in the newspapers, how could he, a man of below average intelligence, memorize that much detail?

It turns out that De Salvo had a near photographic memory, as testified to by his lawyers Jon Asgeirsson and Tony Troy.

Then there's the issue of victim profiles. Serial killers most often target victims that are of similar type. Yet, in the Boston Strangler case, there are two distinct victim groups, one young, one old. This seems to indicate two separate killers.

But might one of those killers not be De Salvo? Let's consider for a while the Green Man assaults, which started in the midst of the Boston Strangler's murderous campaign. Is it likely that Albert De Salvo could have been, simultaneously, a vicious murderer, and a man who tied up his victims, fondled them and then fled the scene after apologizing for what he'd done? It seems highly unlikely.

All of the above is, of course, circumstantial, but there is physical evidence, too, that exonerates De Salvo, at least in one of the murders. For years, both the De Salvo and Sullivan families fought for the bodies of De Salvo and of Mary Sullivan to be exhumed and for the evidence gathered from the scene to be put through DNA analysis. When this was eventually granted, in 2001, it proved two things; that Sullivan did not die in the way De Salvo described in his confession, and that whoever raped Mary Sullivan, it wasn't Albert De Salvo.

Which leaves us with the question: Who was the Boston Strangler? In all likelihood, the Boston Strangler did not exist, at least not as the serial slayer of 13 women. The evidence suggests at least two killers, one targeting older women, one younger. Some of the murders might not even have been connected to either series.

As to who any of these men might have been, the best evidence we have are the eyewitness descriptions of the man seen near both the Clark and Graff murder scenes. Those eyewitnesses were brought to view De Salvo while he was incarcerated at Bridgewater. Both of them categorically said that De Salvo wasn't the man they'd seen. In fact, they said, the man more closely resembled De Salvo's cellmate, George Nasser.

Ted Bundy

The Coed Killer

"I'm the most cold-hearted son of a bitch you'll ever meet."
Ted Bundy

Ted Bundy is the archetypal serial killer, the ultimate bogeyman, a killer so depraved, his deeds so horrific, that even he refused to speak of some of them. And yet, Bundy was no raving lunatic, no salivating madman. This handsome, urbane and intelligent young man was an exemplary student, a volunteer on a suicide hotline, a rising star in the local Republican party. He even earned a commendation from Seattle Police for saving the life of a toddler.

How then do we reconcile these two disparate realities? Bundy himself spoke of "the entity," an evil alter ego that drove him to commit multiple murder. But perhaps that was a ruse, a typical serial killer's ploy to shift the blame to anyone but himself. You be the judge.

Theodore Robert Cowell was born in Burlington, Vermont on November 24, 1946. His mother, Louise Cowell was unmarried, and Ted never knew his biological father. Instead, he was brought up in the home of his grandparents and led to believe that they were his parents and that his mother was his older sister.

At the age of four, Ted and Louise moved to Tacoma, Washington to live with relatives. A year after the move, Louise married a military cook named Johnnie Bundy, and Ted assumed his stepfather's last name. The couple would have four other children. Johnnie Bundy tried hard to bond with his stepson, but Ted preferred to be alone. Years later he'd describe his stepfather as "not very bright."

Ted was a shy boy, uncomfortable in the company of others. Often, this shyness led to him being teased or bullied, but he did well in school, maintaining a high grade-point average. He was more outgoing at Woodrow Wilson High School, where former classmates described him as "well known and well liked." However, Ted had few real friends and seldom dated. He preferred to spend his time at extra-curricular activities like skiing.

After high school, Ted attended the University of Puget Sound and the University of Washington, working at several menial jobs to pay his way. In the spring of 1967, he became romantically involved with UW classmate, Stephanie Brooks, a beautiful and sophisticated young woman from a wealthy Californian family. Ted was deeply in love, but although Stephanie was very fond of him, she found Ted to be immature, lacking in direction and having no specific, future goals - not marriage material in other words.

Shortly after graduating in 1968, she broke off the relationship, leaving Ted devastated.

To make matters worse, in 1969 Bundy learned the truth about his parentage -that his "sister" was actually his mother and his "parents," were actually his grandparents. This must have been traumatic, but outwardly, Bundy's attitude towards his mother did not seem to change much. The impact was seen more in an escalation of Bundy's petty criminality. Through high school and college, many people close to him suspected him of thievery. Now he upped the ante, graduating from minor thefts to shoplifting to burglary. His personality changed too, he became more dominant, more driven. He re-enrolled at UW, as a psychology major, became an honor student, and was well liked by his professors.

It was around this time that Bundy met Elizabeth Kloepfer a divorcée who worked at the university as a secretary. Their relationship would endure long after Bundy was a suspect in a series of murders.

In 1971, Bundy took a job at Seattle's Suicide Hotline crisis center, where he worked alongside former Seattle police officer and future best-selling crime writer, Ann Rule. Rule's recollection of Bundy from this time is that he was "kind, solicitous, and empathetic."

Bundy's life during this period appeared to be on the up. He began sending out applications to various law schools, while his interest in politics saw him work on Washington Governor, Daniel J. Evans', re-election campaign.

In 1973, while on a trip to California on Republican Party business, Bundy met up with Stephanie Brooks, the girlfriend who had dumped him. She was amazed by his transformation to a serious and dedicated young man with a seemingly distinguished legal and political career ahead of him. Bundy began courting her and even brought up the subject of marriage. In January 1974, however, he abruptly broke off the relationship, refusing to take Stephanie's phone calls or answer her letters. Months later, she eventually managed to reach him by phone. When she demanded to know why he had unilaterally ended the relationship, Bundy insisted that he didn't know what she was talking about, then hung up. She never heard from him again.

Within a month of that conversation, young women started to disappear in the Pacific Northwest.

No one knows for certain when Bundy committed his first murder, but of the attacks definitely attributed to him, the first occurred on January 4, 1974. At around midnight, Bundy entered the basement apartment of 18-year-old Karen Sparks, a student at UW. He bludgeoned the sleeping woman with a metal rod from her bed frame, then sexually assaulted her with the same object, causing extensive internal injury. Sparks survived the attack but suffered permanent brain damage.

A month later, Bundy broke into the home of Lynda Ann Healy, a UW undergraduate. He beat her unconscious, then dressed her and carried her away with him. In March, Donna Manson, a 19-year-old student at Evergreen State College in Olympia left her dorm to attend a jazz concert on campus. She never arrived. In April, Susan

Rancourt disappeared while on her way from an evening advisors' meeting at Central Washington State College in Ellensburg. On May 6, Roberta Parks left her dormitory at Oregon State University in Corvallis. Parks was meant to meet some friends for coffee but she never arrived.

As detectives from the King County Sheriff's Office and the Seattle Police Department began investigating the disappearances, they grew increasingly concerned. The women had disappeared without a trace, leaving behind no physical evidence. The only clue seemed to be a man spotted near two of the crimes scenes. He had his arm in a sling and had asked several female students for help carrying some books to his tan Volkswagen Beetle.

On June 1, Brenda Ball, 22, disappeared after leaving a bar in Burien, near Seattle-Tacoma International Airport. She was last seen in the parking lot, talking to a man who had his arm in a sling. In the early hours of June 11, UW student Georgeann Hawkins vanished while walking down a brightly lit alley that ran between her boyfriend's dorm and her sorority house. Again, witnesses reported seeing a man nearby, on crutches with a leg cast, and struggling to carry a briefcase. One woman said that he had asked her to help carry the case to a light-brown Volkswagen Beetle.

With reports of the six missing women creating panic among the student communities in Washington and Oregon, investigators were stumped as to the identity of the perpetrator. All they had were reports of the young man wearing a cast or a sling, and driving a brown or tan Volkswagen Beetle. And even as they fretted, Bundy pulled off his most audacious crime yet, abducting two women from a crowded beach in broad daylight.

The incident occurred on July 14 at Lake Sammamish State Park in Issaquah, 20 miles east of Seattle. Five female witnesses described being approached by a handsome young man with his left arm in a sling, who introduced himself as "Ted." He asked for help in unloading a sailboat from his tan colored Volkswagen Beetle. Four of the women refused; one accompanied him as far as his car but fled when she saw that there was no sailboat. Three other witnesses saw the same man approach 23-year-old Janice Anne Ott, and watched her leave the beach with him. Some four hours later, Denise Naslund, an 18-year-old student, left her friends to go to the restroom and never returned. Bundy later confessed that Ott was still alive when he returned with Naslund, and that one was forced to watch the other being killed.

With a detailed description of the suspect and his car, the King's County Sheriff's Department distributed fliers throughout the Seattle area. A composite sketch was also printed in local newspapers and broadcast on TV. Four separate people - Elizabeth Kloepfer, Ann Rule, a work colleague of Bundy's, and one of his former professors at UW, reported Ted Bundy as a possible suspect. The reports were filed with all the others - the clean-cut law student with no criminal record was not considered a high probability suspect.

On September 6, a couple of grouse hunters found the skeletal remains of Janice Ott, Denise Naslund and another female (later identified as Georgeann Hawkins) about 2 miles east of Lake Sammamish. Six months later the skulls of Lynda Ann Healy, Susan Rancourt, Roberta Parks, and Brenda Ball were found on Taylor Mountain, just east of Issaquah. All showed extensive damage from blunt instrument trauma.

In August 1974, Bundy moved to Salt Lake City to begin his studies at the University of Utah Law School. A new series of homicides began soon after. On September 2, Bundy raped and strangled a still-unidentified hitchhiker in Idaho, disposing of her corpse in a nearby river. On October 2, he abducted 16-year-old Nancy Wilcox in Holladay, dragging her into a wooded area, raping and strangling her to death.

On October 18, Melissa Smith, the 17-year-old daughter of the Midvale police chief, vanished after leaving a pizza parlor. Her naked body was found in the nearby mountains nine days later. Another 17-year-old, Laura Ann Aime, went missing on October 31. Her nude body was found by hikers in American Fork Canyon on Thanksgiving Day. Both women had been beaten, raped, sodomized, and strangled with nylon stockings. Years later Bundy would describe how he returned to the corpses to shampoo their hair and apply makeup.

On November 8, 1974, 18-year-old Carol DaRonch was browsing at a bookstore in a Midvale mall when a man approached her. He identified himself as "Officer Roseland" and told her that someone had tried to break into her vehicle.

DaRonch accompanied the man outside but assured him that nothing had been taken. Nonetheless, "Roseland," insisted that she go with him to the station to file a complaint. She was suspicious, though, when she saw his car. It seemed unlikely that a police officer would be driving a VW Beetle. DaRonch demanded to see his ID, at which "Roseland" produced a detective's gold shield. As they drove away, she realized they were going the wrong way, but

when she pointed this out, the man pulled over and tried to
handcuff her. DaRonch screamed and resisted and, in the struggle
that ensued the man inadvertently fastened both handcuffs to the
same wrist, allowing her to get out of the door and escape.

With the police now looking for him for the attempted abduction,
you might have thought that Bundy would have laid low. Yet, with
astounding audacity, he abducted 17-year-old student, Debra Kent,
from a school play at Viewmont High School that same evening.
The school's drama teacher and another student later told police
about a man who had tried to lure them into the parking lot under
the pretense of looking at a car. Outside the auditorium,
investigators found a key that fit the handcuffs placed on Carol
DaRonch's wrist.

In November, Elizabeth Kloepfer repeated her suspicions about
Bundy to both King County and Salt Lake City investigators. Bundy,
meanwhile, had shifted his hunting ground eastward, towards
Colorado. On January 12, 1975, 23-year-old Caryn Campbell
disappeared from the Wildwood Inn in Snowmass Village,
Colorado, some 400 miles southeast of Salt Lake City. Her naked
body was found a month later. She had been killed by blows to her
head from a blunt instrument On March 15, Julie Cunningham, a
26-year-old ski instructor, disappeared while walking from her
apartment to meet a friend for dinner. Bundy later confessed to
killing her at a site some 90 miles from where she'd been
abducted. Weeks later he drove six hours from Salt Lake City in
order to revisit her corpse.

The next victim was Denise Oliverson, a 25-year-old who
disappeared from Grand Junction, Colorado. Oliverson's bicycle

and sandals were later found under a railroad bridge. On May 6, Bundy kidnapped 12-year-old Lynette Culver from Alameda Junior High School in Pocatello, Idaho. He drowned the girl, then sexually assaulted her corpse in his hotel room. Later, he disposed of her body in the Snake River, north of Pocatello.

On June 28, Susan Curtis disappeared from the campus of Brigham Young University in Provo. Bundy confessed to this murder just before his execution. Curtis' body, like the bodies of Nancy Wilcox, Debbie Kent, Julie Cunningham, Lynette Culver, and Denise Oliverson, has never been found.

Bundy's luck, though, was about to run out. On August 16, 1975, Sergeant Bob Hayward of the Utah Highway Patrol, pulled over a VW Beetle in a routine traffic stop. A search of the vehicle produced a number of suspicious items; a ski mask, another mask made from pantyhose, a crowbar, handcuffs, trash bags, a coil of rope, and an ice pick. Bundy was taken in for questioning, but had ready explanations for all of the items, and with nothing concrete to hold him on, he was released.

However, Detective Jerry Thompson remembered Bundy's name from the call Elizabeth Kloepfer's had made in December 1974. He also believed that Bundy was a good match for the suspect described in the DaRonch abduction. He, therefore, ordered Bundy placed under 24-hour surveillance.

In September, Bundy sold his Volkswagen Beetle to a Midvale teenager. Utah detectives immediately impounded the vehicle and went through it, searching for any minute trace of evidence. They found hairs that could be matched to Caryn Campbell, Melissa Smith, and Carol DaRonch. Based on this, they pulled Bundy in again.

On October 2, 1975, Bundy was put into a lineup and Carol DaRonch immediately picked him out as the man who had assaulted her. The teacher and student who he'd approached at Viewmont High School also identified him as the stranger lurking in the school auditorium the night Debra Kent disappeared. However, there was little evidence to charge him with Kent's disappearance. He was charged instead with the aggravated kidnapping and attempted criminal assault of Carol DaRonch.

That is not to say that investigators were dropping Bundy as a suspect in the murders and disappearances. In November, Detectives Jerry Thompson of Utah, Robert Keppel of Washington, and Michael Fisher of Colorado got together with 30 detectives and prosecutors from various jurisdictions. The purpose of the Aspen Summit was to exchange information on their open cases, and they went away convinced that Bundy was the elusive serial killer they sought. However, there was a frustrating lack of concrete evidence against him and the investigators knew they'd have difficulty making a murder charge stick.

In February 1976, Bundy went on trial for the kidnapping of Carol DaRonch and pulled a 15-year prison term in the Utah State Prison. In October, Colorado authorities charged him with Caryn Campbell's murder and began extradition proceedings.

On June 7, 1977, Bundy was transported to Pitkin County Courthouse in Aspen for a preliminary hearing in the Campbell case. Bundy chose to act as his own attorney, meaning that he was excused by the judge from wearing handcuffs or ankle shackles. He used this to his full advantage, escaping through a window in the courthouse's law library during a recess. Bundy sprained his right ankle during his jump to freedom, but he still managed to make it out of town and into the Aspen Mountains before the alarm was raised. He spent six days on the run, eventually stealing a car and driving back into Aspen where he was re-captured.

Bundy was returned to the prison at Glenwood Springs. Meanwhile, the state's murder case (never that strong to begin with) was falling apart. There is every chance that Bundy would have been acquitted and, with only 18 months to serve on his kidnapping conviction, he'd likely have walked away a free man. Other jurisdictions would also have been discouraged from bringing murder charges against him given their scant evidence.

But Bundy had other ideas. On December 30, while most of the jail staff were on their Christmas break, he escaped again. This time, he managed to crawl into an air-conditioning duct and work his way to a trapdoor that opened into the chief jailer's apartment. Then he simply changed into street clothes and walked out of the front door to freedom. By the time prison staff realized he was missing, Bundy had already driven a stolen car to Denver and taken a flight from there to Chicago.

Bundy's next move was south. Using a combination of stolen vehicles and buses, he worked his way to Ann Arbor, Michigan, then to Atlanta, Georgia and finally to Tallahassee, Florida, arriving on January 8.

According to Bundy, his intention was to go straight, get a legitimate job and keep a low profile in Florida. However, his one attempt at applying for employment met with failure when he was required to provide identification. Soon after, he reverted to petty thievery, shoplifting and credit card theft. It didn't take long, either, for the murderous Bundy to re-emerge.

During the early hours of January 15, 1978, Bundy broke into the Chi Omega sorority house at Florida State University. There, he bludgeoned 21-year-old Margaret Bowman with an oak log, beating her so severely that her skull was splintered and a portion of her brain was exposed, before strangling her to death with a nylon stocking. He then entered the bedroom of 20-year-old Lisa Levy, beat her unconscious, strangled her, and then viciously attacked her with his teeth, almost severing one of her nipples, and leaving deep bite marks on her buttocks. Levy was also raped and sexually assaulted with a hairspray bottle. But, Bundy wasn't done yet. In the adjoining room, he attacked Kathy Kleiner, breaking her jaw and causing deep lacerations to her shoulder; then he turned his attention to Kleiner's roommate Karen Chandler, beating her so savagely that he shattered her jaw and knocked several teeth from her mouth.

Meanwhile, Nita Neary was returning to the sorority house after attending a party. She found the front door standing open. Hearing footsteps ascending the stairs, she hid in the shadows and saw a man with a ski mask pulled over his eyes, exit the building. He was carrying a bloodstained log. Neary immediately alerted the housemother, and a search turned up the carnage Bundy had wrought.

Yet, even as the police were called and were racing to the scene, Bundy's bloodlust was not sated. After leaving the sorority house he broke into a basement apartment eight blocks away and attacked FSU student Cheryl Thomas, fracturing her skull and jaw and leaving her with permanent deafness, and equilibrium damage that ended her dance career.

Bundy next showed up on February 8, driving a white van in Jacksonville, Florida. He tried to lure 14-year-old Leslie Parmenter, the daughter of the Jacksonville PD's Chief of Detectives but fled when Parmeter's brother arrived to pick her up. That same afternoon, he was in Lake City. The following morning, Bundy abducted 12-year-old Kimberley Leach from Lake City Junior High School. Leach's decomposing remains were found seven weeks later, discarded in a disused pig shed near Suwannee River State Park, some 35 miles away.

On February 12, with his cash running low and afraid that the police may be closing in on him, Bundy decided to leave Tallahassee. He stole a car and headed west. Three days later, at around 1:00 a.m., Pensacola police officer David Lee spotted an orange VW Beetle driving erratically near the Alabama state line. A check showed the car to be stolen and the officer pulled Bundy over and placed him under arrest. A struggle ensued during which Bundy swept Lee's legs out from under him and made a run for it. Lee fired two shots before running after Bundy, tackling him to the ground and eventually subduing him. He had no idea that he'd just captured America's most notorious serial killer.

Ted Bundy stood trial for the Chi Omega murders in June 1979.
Despite having access to five court-appointed attorneys, Bundy
again insisted on handling his own defense, sabotaging the entire
process in the opinion of his legal team.

According to public defender Mike Minerva, Bundy was offered a
plea bargain deal that would have saved him from the electric
chair but turned it down because he believed that he could win the
case. He was very wrong. Based largely on forensic evidence
relating to the bite marks he left on Lisa Levy's body, Bundy was
found guilty and sentenced to death. Six months later he received
another death penalty for the murder of Kimberly Leach.

Bundy was sent to the penitentiary at Starke, Florida to await
execution. But there was still the long appeals process to get
through and while this was in process, Bundy consented to a series
of interviews with Stephen Michaud and Hugh Aynesworth. Bundy
spoke in the third person during these interviews, to ensure that
they could not be regarded as confessions, but the content is an
incredible insight into the mind of a serial killer. He spoke of his
descent from shoplifter to burglar to peeping tom and eventually
to murderer, of his need to "totally possess" his victims and of the
terrible deeds he performed on them, both ante and post mortem.
He spoke of revisiting the bodies to perform sexual acts on them
until putrefaction forced him to stop, of decapitating several of his
victims and keeping their severed heads in his apartment.

Later, in interviews with Washington investigator Robert Kessel
and FBI profiler William Hagmaier, Bundy confessed to a total of

30 murders, although Keppel himself believes the real number is much higher, possibly as high as 100.

Eventually, with all appeals and stays exhausted, Ted Bundy went to Florida's electric chair on January 24, 1989. Those present say that he was so paralyzed with fear that he was unable to walk and had to be carried to 'Old Sparky.'

While an estimated crowd of 2, 000 waited outside the prison, Bundy was announced dead at 7:16 a.m. EST, sparking wild celebrations and a fireworks display. One of America's most heinous serial killers was dead, but for his surviving victims, and for the families of those he'd slain, the nightmares will last a lifetime.

Dean Corll

The Candy Man

At around 8:25 on the morning of Wednesday, August 8, 1973, the dispatcher at the police department in Pasadena, Texas, received a frantic phone call. The caller identified himself as Elmer Wayne Henley and told the dispatcher that he'd killed a man. He gave his address as 2020 Lamar Drive and was told to wait there. A unit was immediately sent to the scene.

When the officers arrived, they saw three teenagers, two boys and a girl, standing in front of the house. One of the boys – a timid, skinny youth with a scraggly goatee beard, stepped forward. He said that he had made the call and confessed to being the shooter. The man he'd shot was named Dean Corll. Henley claimed he had fired in self-defense.

After taking a .22 pistol from Henley, the officer placed him and the other two teens (identified as Rhonda Williams and Tim Kerley) into the patrol car. He then entered the residence and found the body of a man, six-foot tall and muscular. He'd been shot six times, bullets lodging in his chest, shoulder and head. The officer returned to the car and read Henley his Miranda rights. Then he summoned crime scene investigators and took the three teenagers in for questioning.

At this point, it looked like a drink and drug-induced homicide, an altercation between friends that had gone wrong. Detectives would soon learn that it was much more than that. They were about to be immersed in the biggest case of serial homicide in US history.

The first indicator should have been the house itself, in particular, the bedroom with its plastic sheeting covering the floors and a sinister plywood board equipped with handcuffs, ropes and cords. Then there was the large hunting knife, the collection of dildos, the duct tape, rolls of plastic, glass tubes and petroleum jelly. If that wasn't enough, they found a coffin-shaped plywood box, with air holes drilled in it and strands of human hair inside.

But the real revelation came back at police headquarters, where Wayne Henley soon made a stunning admission. He said that Dean Corll was a homosexual and a pedophile and that over the last three years, he (Henley) along with another youth named David Brooks, had procured dozens of teenaged boys for Corll. Corll had then raped and tortured these boys before murdering them and disposing of their bodies at a number of burial sites.

The police were initially skeptical of Henley's claims, assuming that he was trying to justify his claim of self-defense in the shooting of Corll. But Henley was insistent, and when he started mentioning the names of some of Corll's victims, officers sat up and took notice. The names were familiar to them, all of the boys had been reported missing over the last few years. Furthermore, Henley said he could take the officers to four separate burial sites. If the numbers Henley was quoting were accurate, it would make Dean Corll the worst mass murderer in American history.

Dean Arnold Corll was born on December 24, 1939, in Fort Wayne, Indiana. His father, Arnold was strict with his son, his mother, Mary, tended to be overprotective. The marriage was not a happy one and, in 1946, the couple divorced. A reconciliation in 1950 ended in divorce again, three years later.

Dean went to stay with his mother, but his parents remained on amicable terms and Dean and his younger brother Simon remained in regular contact with their father. After the second divorce, Corll's mother married a traveling salesman by the name of Jake West and the family moved to the small town of Vidor, Texas. Not long after, Mary started a small candy company named 'Pecan Prince.' Dean and his brother were actively involved in the business, running the candy making machines and packing the produce, which Jake West would sell on his sales route.

Corll's mother divorced Jake West in 1963 and started a new business, 'Corll Candy Company.' Dean was drafted into the US Army that year and served 10 months before successfully applying for a hardship discharge, on the grounds that he was needed in the family business.

In 1965, the Corll Candy Company relocated to new premises, across the street from Helms Elementary School. It was here that

Corll first acquired his infamous nickname, "The Candy Man," due to his habit of giving free candy to local children, particularly teenaged boys. The company also employed a few local kids, and Corll was known to flirt with teenage male employees. He even installed a pool table in a back room, which became a hangout for local youths. It was here that he met 12-year-old David Brooks in 1967.

Brooks was initially just one of many boys who hung out in the room behind the store, but over time Corll became more and more attentive to him, giving him gifts of money and taking him on trips to various beaches. When Brooks parents divorced, he went to live with his mother in Beaumont, 85 miles away. But when he visited his father in Houston, he often spent time at Corll's apartment. In 1970, when Brooks was 15, he and Corll became involved in a sexual relationship.

At around this time, Corll's mother moved to Colorado and, following the closure of the candy business, Corll found work as an electrician with the Houston Lighting and Power Company. He'd remain employed there until his death.

It is impossible to say what turned Dean Corll from a seemingly diligent, caring, young man to a sadistic torturer and murderer of teenaged boys. He did seem to have an unhealthy interest in boys half his age and was most likely a pedophile. Still, as despicable as the acts of that particular breed of criminal are, few of them are mass murderers. And Dean Corll was about to embark on a deadly campaign.

The first known victim was an 18-year-old college freshman, named Jeffrey Konen, who disappeared while hitchhiking on September 25, 1970. He was last seen at the corner of Westheimer Road in the Uptown area of Houston, close to where Corll was living at the time. He'd be found, three years later, in a shallow grave at High Island Beach.

Brooks claimed that around this time he walked in on Corll assaulting two teenaged boys. Corll promised Brooks a car in return for his silence and also made a standing offer of $200 for any youths Brooks was able to lure to Corll's apartment. Brooks accepted both proposals, receiving a green Chevrolet Corvette, and soon after, procuring two 14-year-olds for Corll.

The boys, James Glass and Danny Yates, had been attending a religious rally in the Heights district of Houston when David Brooks approached them and asked if they wanted to hang out with him and drink some beer. Glass was a friend of Brooks who'd been to Corll's apartment before, so they readily agreed. Once there, Corll overpowered them, cuffed them to his torture board and then raped and tortured them before strangling them to death. He and Brooks later buried them beneath a boatshed that Corll had recently rented.

Six weeks after the murder of Glass and Yates, Brooks and Corll saw two teenage brothers named Donald and Jerry Waldrop walking towards a bowling alley. The boys were enticed into Corll's van, then driven to Corll's apartment, where they were raped, tortured, strangled and subsequently buried in the boat shed.

Three more victims followed between March and May 1971. Fifteen-year-old Randell Harvey was abducted while cycling to his part-time job as a gas station attendant. He was killed by a single bullet to the head. David Hilligiest, 13, and Gregory Winkle, 16, were friends who were abducted and killed together on the afternoon of May 29, 1971. Soon after their disappearances, the parents of all three boys launched a frantic, but ultimately fruitless, search for their sons. All three would be found buried under Corll's boatshed in 1973.

On August 17, 1971, Corll and Brooks were out cruising when they spotted 17-year-old Ruben Watson Haney walking home from a movie. Like James Glass, Haney was a friend of David Brooks, and Brooks persuaded him to attend a party at Corll's new apartment on San Felipe Street. Haney accompanied the pair to Corll's home where he was strangled and then buried in the boat shed.

In September 1971, Corll moved again, this time to 915 Columbia Street. Two more youths were murdered at this address according to Brooks, although their identities remain unknown.

The next teenager that Brooks procured for Corll was Elmer Wayne Henley. However, for some unexplained reason, perhaps because he saw a kindred spirit, Corll decided not to kill Henley. Instead, he made Henley the same offer he'd made David Brooks - $200 for any boy he could lure to Corll's apartment.

According to Henley, he initially rejected Corll's offer. But, early in 1972, with his family in desperate need of money, he finally gave in. Corll was by now living at 925 Schuler Street, and Henley said that he and Corll picked up a youth and asked him if he wanted to join them in drinking beer and smoking pot. The boy agreed and once at the house they restrained him using a ruse he and Corll had practiced beforehand. Henley cuffed his own hands behind his back, then freed himself using a key hidden in his back pocket. He then persuaded the youth to try it, but once his hands were cuffed, Henley walked out, leaving the boy alone with Corll.

The identity of this victim is not known, but it may have been Willard Branch, a 17-year-old who disappeared on February 9, 1972, and who was later found buried beneath the boatshed.

One month later, on March 24, 1972, Corll, working with both of his young accomplices, persuaded 18-year-old Frank Aguirre (an acquaintance of Henley) to drink beer and smoke marijuana with them. Aguirre agreed and followed the trio to Corll's home where Corll overpowered him and cuffed his hands behind his back.

Henley later claimed that he tried to persuade Corll not to kill Aguirre, but Corll refused. Nonetheless, Henley accepted his $200 payment and helped Corll and Brooks bury Aguirre at High Island Beach.

On April 20, 1972, Henley led another friend of his to his death at the hands of Dean Corll. Seventeen-year-old Mark Scott fought furiously for his life, but when Corll produced a gun he "just gave up" according to Henley. Scott was tied to the torture board and suffered the same fate as Frankie Aguirre. He was raped, tortured and strangled, then buried at High Island Beach.

According to Brooks, Henley wasn't just a procurer for Corll, but an active and sadistic participant in the murders, especially those that occurred at Schuler Street. Before Corll moved from the address on June 26, Henley helped Corll and Brooks to abduct and murder two youths, Billy Baulch and Johnny Delone. In Brooks' later confession, he said that both boys were tied to Corll's bed and, after being tortured and raped, Henley manually strangled Baulch to death. He then shouted, "Hey, Johnny!" before shooting Delone in the head. The bullet exited through Delone's ear but didn't kill him. Then, as he pleaded for his life, Henley strangled him to death.

Another youth who was lured to Corll's Schuler Street residence was 19-year-old Billy Ridinger. Like the other victims, Ridinger was tied to the board, tortured and raped by Corll. However, Brooks claimed that he persuaded Corll to let Ridinger go. On another occasion, Brooks feared that he might, himself, become a victim. Henley knocked him unconscious as he entered the house, and he woke to find himself tied to Corll's bed. Corll raped him repeatedly but later released him. Despite the assault, Brooks continued to help Corll in the abduction of the victims.

Corll next moved to an apartment at Westcott Towers, where he is known to have killed two more victims. The first of these was 17-year-old Steven Sickman, last seen leaving a party just after midnight on July 20. He was savagely beaten with a blunt instrument before being strangled to death and buried in the boat shed. A month later, Roy Bunton, 19, was abducted while walking to work. He was shot twice in the head and was also buried in the boat shed.

Less than two months later, on October 2, 1972, Henley and Brooks persuaded two teenagers named Wally Jay Simoneaux and Richard Hembree to join them at Corll's apartment. That evening, Simoneaux's mother received a strange call from her son. He spoke only one word into the phone, a plaintive "Mama," before the connection was terminated. The next morning, Henley accidently shot Hembree in the mouth and several hours later, both boys were strangled to death. They were buried in the boat shed, their bodies placed on top of those of James Glass and Danny Yates. The following month, a 19-year-old youth named Richard Kepner was abducted and murdered, then buried at High Island Beach.

On January 20, 1973, Corll moved to Wirt Road in the Spring Branch district of Houston. Within two weeks of moving to this address, he killed a 17-year-old named Joseph Lyles, a friend of both Brooks and Corll. On March 7, Corll moved from Wirt Road to an address his father had recently vacated, 2020 Lamar Drive, Pasadena.

There were no further murders between February and June 3, 1973, although Corll is known to have been ill during this time and Henley was out of town, having moved to Mount Pleasant in an apparent effort to get away from Corll. When the killings did start up again, they started with a vengeance, and both Brooks and Henley would later testify that Corll had become more brutal than ever. His two accomplices had learned to recognize when Corll was getting ready to kill. He'd become reckless, smoking constantly and displaying twitchy reflex movements. Soon after, he'd announce that he "needed to do a new boy," and the unholy trio would hit the streets in search of victims.

On June 4, Henley and Corll abducted a 15-year-old named William Ray Lawrence. They raped and tortured the boy for three days before burying him at Lake Sam Rayburn. Less than two weeks later, 20-year-old Raymond Blackburn was abducted, strangled and buried at the same location. Corll was accelerating now. On July 7, Homer Garcia, 15, an acquaintance of Henley's was shot, then left to bleed to death in Corll's bathtub and on July 12, a 17-year-old youth named John Sellars was shot to death and buried at High Island Beach.

In July 1973, David Brooks married his pregnant fiancée, and Henley temporarily became Corll's sole accomplice. Three more teenagers would die between July 19 and July 25; 15-year-old Michael Baulch was strangled and buried at Lake Sam Rayburn; Charles Cobble and Marty Ray Jones were abducted together and buried in the boat shed. These were the only abductions in which David Brooks did not play a part.

The last to die was also Corll's youngest victim. James Dreymala was just 13 years old when he was snatched from his bicycle on August 3, 1973. He was tied to Corll's torture board, raped, tortured and strangled before being buried in the boat shed.

Four days later, Dean Corll would be dead, shot during an altercation with one of his own accomplices.

On the evening of August 7, 1973, Henley brought a 19-year-old named Timothy Kerley to Corll's house in Pasadena, intending for him to be Corll's next victim. The two drank beer and sniffed paint until around midnight when they went to buy something to eat.

While they were out, Kerley suggested picking up 15-year-old Rhonda Williams, a friend of both youths. Rhonda agreed to accompany them, but when they arrived, Corll was furious that Henley had brought a girl to his house. Eventually, Henley managed to calm Corll down and he offered the teenagers beer and marijuana. The three began drinking, sniffing paint fumes and smoking pot, while Corll watched them intently. Eventually, they passed out.

Henley woke lying on his stomach with Corll snapping handcuffs onto his wrists. His mouth had been taped shut and his ankles bound together. Kerley and Williams lay beside Henley, securely bound and gagged, Kerley stripped naked.

Noticing that Henley was awake, Corll removed the gag from his mouth. He told Henley that he was going to kill all three of them after he'd raped and tortured Kerley. He then started kicking Rhonda Williams in the chest, then dragged Henley into the kitchen and placed a gun to his stomach, threatening to shoot him. Henley managed to calm Corll down by promising to help torture and murder Williams and Kerley. Corll then uncuffed Henley, and the two of them carried Kerley and Williams to the bedroom and tied them to the torture board.

Corll instructed Henley to cut away Rhonda's clothes and rape her while he did likewise to Kerley. He began torturing and assaulting Kerley. Henley then asked Corll if he could take Rhonda into another room and when Corll ignored him, Henley suddenly grabbed Corll's gun.

"I can't go on any longer!" Henley shouted. "I can't have you kill all my friends!"

"Kill me, Wayne!" Corll said. Then, as he advanced towards Henley, "You won't do it!"

Henley fired one shot, hitting Corll in the forehead, then as Corll lurched forward, he fired twice more, striking Corll's left shoulder. Corll spun round and staggered towards the door before Henley fired three more shots into his lower back and shoulder. Henley then released Kerley and Williams and after some discussion, they called the police.

The monster was dead, but police still had to find closure for the families of the victims.

Wayne Henley led police to Corll's boat shed, where he claimed most of the victims were buried. As they began digging they soon uncovered the body of a young blond-haired boy, lying on his side, wrapped in clear plastic and buried beneath a layer of lime. As the evacuations continued more remains were found, in varying stages of decomposition. Some victims had been shot, others strangled, the ligatures still wrapped tightly around their necks.

All of the victims had been sodomized and most bore clear evidence of sexual torture: pubic hairs plucked out, genitals chewed, objects inserted into their rectums, glass rods shoved into their penises and smashed. In many cases, rags had been inserted into the victims' mouths and secured with adhesive tape to muffle their screams. In some instances, Corll had castrated his live victims: severed genitals were found inside a number of sealed plastic bags.

On August 8, 1973, a total of eight corpses were uncovered at the boatshed. That same day David Brooks handed himself over to the Houston Police. He denied participating in any of the murders, saying only that he knew of two murders Corll had committed in 1970.

The following day, August 9, Henley gave a written statement detailing his and Brooks' involvement and there were nine more bodies recovered from the boat shed. Henley also accompanied police officers to Lake Sam Rayburn in San Augustine County, where two more bodies were found in shallow graves.

Faced with the mounting evidence against him, David Brooks gave a full confession that evening, admitting to being present at several of the murders and helping with several of the burials. He continued to deny direct participation in the killings.

On August 10, two more bodies were found buried at Lake Sam Rayburn and police began their search at High Island Beach, where two more victims were found, interred in shallow graves. Three days later, Henley and Brooks again accompanied the police to High Island Beach, where four more bodies were found, taking the total of twenty-seven known victims – at the time the worst killing spree in American history.

Elmer Wayne Henley and David Owen Brooks were tried separately for their roles in the murders. Henley was brought to trial in San Antonio on July 1, 1974, charged with six murders. He was found guilty and sentenced to six consecutive 99-year terms - a total of 594 years – meaning he will never see the outside of a prison cell.

David Brooks stood trial on February 27, 1975, accused of four murders committed between December 1970 and June 1973. He was found guilty on one charge and sentenced to life imprisonment without the possibility of parole.

Jeffrey Dahmer

The Milwaukee Cannibal

"It is hard for me to believe that a human being could have done what I have done." Jeffrey Dahmer

Bundy, Gacy, and Dahmer, an unholy trinity who are arguably the three most notorious serial killers in American history. Of these, Dahmer remains the most enigmatic, his crimes the most bizarre. A seemingly normal young man possessed of a morbid and unwholesome fascination with the dead, a necrophile, cannibal, amateur taxidermist and performer of makeshift lobotomies. Jeffrey Dahmer was all of these things. Even then, we are only just scratching the surface.

At around 2 a.m. on the morning of May 27, 1991, Milwaukee PD received a report of a young Asian boy running naked along North 25th Street. Officers were dispatched to the scene and found the dazed boy being treated by paramedics. Also present were Sandra Smith, 18, her cousin Nicole Childress, also 18, and a tall, blonde man. Smith was the one who had called the police. She and the man were engaged in a heated argument.

As the officers stepped between them, the man identified himself as Jeffrey Dahmer. He said that, despite his youthful looks, the boy was 19-years-old, that his name was Konerak, and that the two of them were lovers. He said that Konerak had had too much to drink and apologized for the trouble he had caused.

The two young women tried to intervene, insisting that the boy looked much younger than 19, that he had clearly been drugged, and that they had seen him trying to escape from the blond man just before the police arrived. To their dismay, the police were dismissive of their account. They asked Konerak whether he could confirm Dahmer's story, but the boy's reply was incoherent. He seemed dazed, possibly under the influence of drugs.

Nonetheless, the officers appeared willing to accept Dahmer's version of events, although they insisted on escorting him and Konerak back to their apartment. Once there, they asked if they could check inside. Dahmer made no objection. The apartment was exceedingly neat, even though an unpleasant smell, like spoilt meat, hung in the air. As Konerak was led to a sofa, Dahmer again apologized for his behavior and promised that it would not happen again. He was well-spoken and calm, and the officers had no reason to disbelieve his story. Not wanting to become involved in a domestic squabble between homosexual lovers, they left.

Dahmer's calm handling of the situation is remarkable, even for a psychopath. Had the police bothered to check the apartment, they would have found the decomposing corpse of his last victim, Tony Hughes, lying on the bedroom floor. Had they bothered to run a background check, they would have discovered that Jeffrey Dahmer was a convicted child molester who was still on probation. Within minutes of the officers' departure, Dahmer had strangled 14-year-old Konerak to death and was having sex with his corpse.

Two months later, on the oppressively hot evening of July 22, 1991, two Milwaukee police officers, Robert Rauth and Rolf Mueller, were patrolling the high-crime area around Marquette University. At around midnight, they spotted a slim, African American man with a handcuff dangling from his wrist. Assuming that he'd escaped from another police officer, they got out of their cruiser and took him into custody.

The man identified himself as Tracy Edwards and then launched into a bizarre tale about the "weird guy" who had tried to put the cuffs on him. He said that when he'd resisted, the man had threatened him with a butcher's knife and forced him into a bedroom where he'd seen pictures on the wall depicting mutilated bodies. He'd also noticed a large blue barrel standing in the corner, which gave off a terrible smell. Certain that he was about to be killed, Edwards had fought for his life. He'd punched the man in the face, kicked him in the stomach, and run for the door.

The officers had heard similar stories before. Usually, they were exaggerated and amounted to a domestic dispute between lovers. Nonetheless, they decided they'd better check it out.

Getting the address from Edwards, they drove to the Oxford Apartments at 924 North 25th Street. The door to Apartment 213 was opened by a tall, blond man who identified himself as Jeffrey Dahmer. He admitted cuffing Edwards but insisted it was part of a game. He offered to get the keys to the cuffs from his bedroom. As he turned to do so, Edwards shouted that the knife Dahmer had used to threaten him was also in the bedroom.

One of the officers then decided to go into the bedroom himself. There, he saw the photographs that Edwards had described, photos of human corpses in various stages of dissection, one showing a head in the refrigerator. He shouted immediately for his partner to place Dahmer under arrest.

Up until this point, Dahmer had been calm and cooperative. Now, as the officer tried to cuff him, he suddenly began fighting and trying to get away. While one officer subdued him, the other went to the refrigerator, noticing that it was the same one shown in the photograph. He angled the door open with trepidation knowing what he was likely to find there. Still, the blank eyes that stared out at him caused him to slam the door shut instantly. "There's a goddamn head in the refrigerator!" he shouted to his partner.

The officers placed Dahmer under arrest and called for backup. Soon, an army of detectives and crime scene investigators had descended on the small apartment. It didn't take long for them to discover the massive scale of the murder spree they'd stumbled upon.

The one-bedroom residence was almost obsessively neat on the surface, but that just served to highlight the horrors lurking beneath. The box of baking soda placed in the refrigerator was hardly enough to absorb the smell of decomposition from the severed head. There was a human heart in the refrigerator too, and three more heads, neatly stored in plastic bags, stashed in the freezer.

In the back of a bedroom closet was a metal stockpot containing decomposed hands and a penis. On the shelf above, was a kettle containing two human skulls.

On other shelves, the police found containers of ethyl alcohol, chloroform, and formaldehyde. There were also glass jars holding male genitalia preserved in formaldehyde. The collection of Polaroid photographs was pinned to the wall. They showed corpses at various stages of dissection. One showed a man's head lying in the kitchen sink, another showed a cadaver cut open from neck to groin. Other photos showed corpses placed in erotic poses.

And then there was the barrel Edwards had described. It was filled with a potent acid that Dahmer had used to dissolve the bodies of his victims into a sludge that he could later flush down the apartment's toilet.

Dahmer had in the meantime been transported to police headquarters for questioning. As he began to recount his incredible tale of murder and mayhem to gape-mouthed detectives, stories began to leak into the media. Soon, lurid tales of necrophilia, cannibalism and Satanism were screaming from the front pages of the nation's newspapers, causing shockwaves that reverberated around the world. What kind of a person could commit such barbarous acts, the public wanted to know. How does a man become a serial killer, a necrophile, and a cannibal? Just who was Jeffrey Dahmer?

Jeffrey Dahmer was born in West Allis, Wisconsin on May 21, 1960. His mother, Joyce, was an office worker, his father, Lionel, a chemistry major at Marquette University. Both parents doted on young Jeffrey, but as he grew up, there were increased tensions in the household. Joyce was neurotic and argumentative, a hypochondriac who became addicted to the prescription drug, Equanil, and once attempted suicide. Lionel spent most of his time at his studies and was often absent from the home.

At school, Dahmer was regarded as quiet and reserved with very few friends. He compensated by developing an interest in animals, initially collecting large insects and keeping them in jars. Later, Dahmer would gather animal carcasses from the roadside, dismember the bodies and store the parts in jars in the family's tool shed. In one instance, he impaled a dog's head on a stake behind his house. Lionel Dahmer would later reject the notion that his son ever killed or tortured animals - a trait common among fledgling serial killers. This actually makes sense. Jeffrey was more interested in dead things.

In October 1966, the Dahmer family relocated to Doylestown, Ohio, where Jeff's younger brother, David, was born on December 18, 1966. The same year, Lionel Dahmer completed his degree and found work as an analytical chemist in Akron.

Dahmer attended Revere High School, where he made average grades. He had few friends and participated in few activities. What he did have, though, was a drinking problem. From about the age of 14, he had been bringing both beer and spirits to school, and drinking before, after and during classes.

By the time he reached puberty, Dahmer was well on the way to being an alcoholic. He also knew that he was a homosexual, although he kept this information to himself. He did have a brief relationship with another youth during his early teens, but the pair never went as far as sexual intercourse.

Dahmer would later admit that from around this time, he began to develop elaborate sexual fantasies, usually involving him being in a dominant position over an entirely subservient partner. Eventually, these fantasies morphed to include his preoccupation with dissection. Dahmer also developed a sexual obsession with a particular male jogger. He concocted a fantasy where he knocked the man out and had sex with his unconscious body. He even went so far as to put his plan into action, but on the day that he concealed himself in bushes holding a baseball bat, the jogger did not pass that way.

Dahmer graduated high school in May 1978. His parent's had divorced the previous year and Joyce had gained custody of David. Jeffrey, having just turned 18, was legally an adult and therefore not subject to custody issues. With his father living in a nearby motel and his mother and brother having relocated to Chippewa Falls, Dahmer was alone in the family home. On June 25, 1978, just three weeks after his graduation, he committed his first murder.

On that day, Dahmer picked up a 19-year-old hitchhiker named
Stephen Hicks. The youth had been on his way to a rock concert in
Lockwood Corners but Dahmer persuaded him to come back to his
house and drink some alcohol. According to Dahmer's later
testimony, the two spent several hours drinking and listening to
music. Eventually, Hicks wanted to leave. In order to prevent him
doing so, Dahmer struck Hicks with a 10-pound dumbbell and
then bludgeoned him to death. He then dissected the body and
buried it in the backyard. Weeks later, he disinterred the remains,
dissolved the flesh in acid and crushed the bones with a
sledgehammer.

Six weeks after the murder, Dahmer's father moved back home,
bringing his new fiancée with him. That August, Dahmer enrolled
at Ohio State University, but he flunked out after just one
semester, mainly as a result of his continuing alcohol abuse. In
January 1979, at his father's urging, he enlisted in the army.

Dahmer was sent to Fort Sam Houston, where he trained as a
medic. Upon completion of his training, he was posted to
Baumholder, Germany. He would spend just over two years in the
military, his tenure passing mainly without incident. However, he
continued drinking heavily, his alcoholism eventually resulting in
him being discharged in March 1981.

Back in the States, Dahmer opted to move to Florida, rather than
return to his father's home. He found employment in a sandwich
shop and rented a room in a nearby motel. But Dahmer's
alcoholism continued to plague him. He spent almost all of his
wages on booze, leading to his eventual eviction from the motel.

Unable to afford accommodation, he lived for a time on the streets before phoning his father and asking if he could return home.

Within two weeks of his return, Dahmer was arrested for being drunk and disorderly and, as his drinking continued to spiral out of control, Lionel Dahmer convinced his son to move to his grandmother's house in West Allis. Dahmer was fond of his grandmother and Lionel believed that the change of scenery would do him good.

At first, it seemed to work. Dahmer began attending church, willingly helped with chores around the house and found employment as a phlebotomist at the Milwaukee Blood Plasma Center. But he continued to drink, and on August 7, 1982, he was arrested for exposing himself to a group of women and children at the Wisconsin State Fair. Not long after, he lost his job. He would remain unemployed for the next two years.

In January 1985, Dahmer was hired as a mixer at the Milwaukee Ambrosia Chocolate Factory, working the 11 p.m. to 7 a.m. shift. At around this time, a seemingly innocuous incident occurred which would trigger Dahmer's descent into madness. According to Dahmer, he was reading at the West Allis Public Library when a stranger passed him a note, offering to perform fellatio on him. Dahmer did not respond, but the incident rekindled his adolescent fantasies of control and dominance. Soon after, he began frequenting gay bars, bookstores, and bathhouses.

By late 1985, Dahmer was a regular on the Milwaukee bathhouse scene. But the sexual encounters he found there frustrated him. By his own admission, he regarded his sexual partners as "objects of pleasure" rather than people. He preferred them to be immobile during the act and to this extent he began feeding them alcohol laced with sleeping tablets. He'd then have sex with them as they lay unconscious. Dahmer later confessed to abusing 12 men in this way, but inevitably, word got out and he found himself banned from the bathhouses.

Rather than stop his activities, Dahmer merely transferred them to a different location. He started taking his partners to hotel rooms, drugging them and then performing sexual acts on their inanimate forms. It was a short step from this "pseudo-necrophilia" to the real thing.

In November 1987, nine years after the murder of Stephen Hicks, Dahmer met 25-year-old Steven Tuomi in a bar and persuaded him to go back to his hotel room. Once there, Dahmer followed his now familiar M.O., drugging Tuomi and having sex with him after he passed out. However, this time, Dahmer did not stop at mere rape.

According to his later account, Dahmer woke the next morning to find Tuomi dead, his chest "crushed in" and blood seeping from his mouth. Dahmer claimed that he had no recollection of killing Tuomi, but knew that he must have done it because his fists were bruised, presumably from striking the man.

Faced with the problem of disposing of the body, Dahmer purchased a large suitcase, which he used to transport the corpse to his grandmother's house. There he dissected it, first severing the head, arms, and legs, then slicing the flesh from the bones and placing the chunks in garbage bags. The bones were wrapped in sheets and pounded to splinters with a sledgehammer. All of the remains were disposed of in the trash, the entire dismemberment taking about two hours to complete.

The killing of Steven Tuomi may have been unintentional, but it whetted Dahmer's appetite for murder. He now began actively seeking out victims, luring them back to his grandmother's home, drugging and then sexually assaulting them before killing them by strangulation.

The next to die was a 15-year-old male prostitute named James Doxtator. Dahmer met the Native American youth two months after the murder of Tuomi. He offered the boy $50 to pose for nude pictures. Doxtator was drugged, strangled and dismembered. On March 24, 1988, 25-year-old Richard Guerrero met a similar fate.

On April 23, Dahmer lured another potential victim to his house, the young man only surviving the encounter because Dahmer's grandmother arrived home unexpectedly.

By September 1988, Dahmer's grandmother had had enough of him bringing home young men late at night and asked him to move out. On September 25, Dahmer moved to a one-bedroom apartment on North Twenty-fifth Street. Just a day later, he was arrested for drugging and sexually assaulting a 13-year-old boy. The case came to trial in January 1989, and Dahmer was sentenced to five years' probation and one year in a work release camp. He was also required to register as a sex offender.

Two months later, Dahmer claimed his fifth victim. Anthony Sears was an aspiring model who met Dahmer at a gay bar on March 25, 1989. According to Dahmer, he wasn't looking for a victim that night, but Sears struck up a conversation with him just as the bar was about to close. Dahmer had by this time temporarily moved back in with his grandmother and he invited Sears to come home with him. After the two engaged in oral sex, Dahmer drugged and strangled Sears. The following morning, he dissected the corpse in the bathtub and disposed of it in the manner which he had by now perfected.

Dahmer later stated that he was strongly attracted to Sears and it is perhaps for this reason that he retained some of his body parts, the first time he had done so. He preserved Sears' skull and genitalia in acetone, storing them in his work locker before he moved them to his new apartment the following year.

In May 1990, Dahmer moved out of his grandmother's house for the final time and took up residence at the address that would later become infamous: Apartment 213, 924 North 25th Street, Milwaukee. Now free of the risk of discovery, he stepped up the pace of his killings, committing four more murders before the end of 1990, two more in February and April 1991, and another in May 1991.

In May 1991, Dahmer had the narrow escape when Konerak Sinthasomphone escaped from his apartment only to be returned to him by the police. Thereafter, Dahmer's killing spree went into overdrive and he began to conduct obscene experiments on his victims.

His plan was to create completely submissive "zombie" sex slaves and to achieve this he began to perform crude "lobotomies." He would drill holes into the skulls of his living victims, then inject hydrochloric acid or boiling water into the frontal lobe area of their brains. When these experiments failed to achieve the desired result, Dahmer simply dispatched the unfortunate victim, harvested whatever trophies he desired from the body and dissolved the rest in his acid vat. He had also by this time begun to indulge in cannibalism, believing that his victims would live on inside him if he consumed their flesh.

Between June and July 1991, Dahmer claimed four victims in the space of just three weeks, murdering Matt Turner on June 30, Jeremiah Weinberger on July 5, Oliver Lacy on July 12, and Joseph Bradehoft on July 19.

It was around this time that other residents of the Oxford Apartments began noticing the bumps and thumps of falling objects from Apartment 213, the occasional buzz or a power saw and, most of all, the vile smells emanating from the apartment. Dahmer's bloodlust was up, his killing spree was accelerating. Who knows how many more young men he might have killed had Tracey Edwards not escaped from his clutches on July 22, 1991.

Jeffrey Dahmer was indicted on 15 murder charges, the matter coming to trial on January 30, 1992. With the overwhelming evidence against him, his defense team saw no other strategy but to plead not guilty by reason of insanity. It was a sensible approach given the immense depravity of the crimes involved. However, it would ultimately prove unsuccessful.

After a trial that lasted two weeks, the jury rejected the insanity plea and returned a guilty verdict on each of the charges. Wisconsin has no death penalty statute on its books, so that was never an option. Instead, Dahmer received 15 life terms, amounting to a total of 957 years in prison.

But Dahmer would serve less than three of those years. On November 28, 1994, while doing janitorial work in the prison gym, he was attacked and severely beaten by fellow inmate Christopher Scarver, who used a metal bar removed from a piece of exercise equipment for the purpose. Dahmer received severe head trauma, ironically similar to the wounds suffered by his first victim, Stephen Hicks. He died in the ambulance on the way to hospital.

Albert Fish

The Werewolf of Wisteria

On Monday, May 28, 1928, Mrs. Delia Budd, answered the door of her apartment to an elderly, kindly looking man. He introduced himself as Frank Howard, a farmer from Long Island, and said he was there in response to an advertisement that Mrs. Budd's 18-year-old son, Edward, had placed in the Sunday edition of the New York World. He was interested in employing the young man to work on his farm.

After a brief interview, Howard said that Edward would be suitable for the position and offered him a salary of $15 per week. Not only that, but he was prepared to employ Edward's best friend, Willie, as well. Hardly able to believe their good fortune, the boys quickly agreed, upon which Howard departed, promising to return on Saturday, June 2, to collect them.

Frank Howard did not return on Saturday, but he did send an apologetic telegram, explaining that he'd been delayed and would call the following day instead. He arrived the next morning at around 11, bringing gifts of strawberries and fresh cheese, explaining they were from his farm.

Mrs. Budd invited the kindly old man to stay to lunch and he readily agreed, spending the pre-meal time in conversation with Mrs. Budd's husband, Albert, and the Budd children. He seemed particularly enthralled, though, by the couple's beautiful 10-year-old daughter, Grace.

After the meal, Howard explained that he had a prior engagement to attend, a birthday party for his niece. He promised to return later that evening to pick up Edward and Willie and gave them $2 to attend the pictures. He also gave the younger Budd children money for candy. Then, as he was leaving, an idea seemed to strike him. If the Budd's were agreeable, he wanted to take Grace to the children's birthday party he was going to attend.

Mrs. Budd was at first dubious, but her husband persuaded her to allow the child to go. After getting the address (137th Street and Columbus Avenue, Howard said), Delia Budd acceded. Grace left the house holding Frank Howard's hand, still dressed in the white confirmation dress she'd worn to church that morning.

Grace did not return home that evening, and the Budd's spent a frantic, sleepless night worrying about their daughter. They tried hard to convince themselves that the party had run later than expected and that Grace had spent the night at Mr. Howard's sister's house. But when the following morning arrived with still no sign of Mr. Howard or the child, Albert Budd decided to go to the police. He was referred to the Missing Persons Bureau and eventually to veteran detective, William King. King was immediately suspicious, as the address given by Howard did not exist (Columbus ran only as far as 109th Street). Further investigation turned up no Frank Howard who owned a farm on Long Island.

An extensive investigation was launched. The police checked out everything Frank Howard had told the Budds, then had the Budds go through reams of mugshots, hoping to find Howard's true identity. It came to nothing.

On June 7, 1,000 fliers were mailed to police stations around the country, giving a photo of Grace Budd and a description of "Frank Howard." All that did was generate a heap of false sightings and useless tips, which had to be checked out by the 20 detectives working the case.

The police did find some clues, though, including the original of the Western Union telegram "Frank Howard" had sent to the Budds and the stall where he'd bought the cheese and strawberries he'd gifted to them. The peddler described the man in detail but couldn't recall anything that would provide investigators with an idea of how to find him. Frank Howard seemed to have disappeared, taking Grace Budd with him.

Despite the best efforts of police, the trail eventually went cold. Detectives were assigned to new cases and the Grace Budd case was assigned to a filing cabinet. No one expected that it would ever be solved. One man, though, refused to give up. Detective William King had been one of the first detectives assigned to the case and he remained determined to catch the fiend who had snatched Grace Budd. King even refused retirement in 1932 so that he could continue working the case.

One of the tactics that King employed was to occasionally use his contacts in the press to plant false stories about a break in the Budd case, hoping to flush the perpetrator out of hiding. One such article was posted in Walter Winchell's column on November 2, 1934. It claimed that the Department of Missing Persons had a break in the case and expected to make an arrest within four weeks.

Ten days later, Delia Budd received a letter so barbarous that it is fortunate her lack of education prevented her from reading it. Her son Edward read it instead and immediately contacted Detective King.

The full transcript of the letter read as follows;

"My dear Mrs. Budd,

In 1894 a friend of mine shipped as a deck hand on the Steamer Tacoma, Capt. John Davis. They sailed from San Francisco for Hong Kong China. On arriving there he and two others went ashore and got drunk. When they returned the boat was gone.

At that time there was famine in China. Meat of any kind was from $1 to $3 a pound. So great was the suffering among the very poor that all children under 12 were sold for food in order to keep others from starving. A boy or girl under 14 was not safe in the street. You could go in any shop and ask for steak — chops — or stew meat. Part of the naked body of a boy or girl would be brought out and just what you wanted cut from it. A boy or girls behind which is the sweetest part of the body and sold as veal cutlet brought the highest price.

John staid there so long he acquired a taste for human flesh. On his return to N.Y. he stole two boys one seven, one 11. Took them to his home stripped them naked tied them in a closet. Then burned everything they had on. Several times every day and night he spanked them — tortured them — to make their meat good and tender.

First he killed the 11-year-old boy, because he had the fattest ass and of course the most meat on it. Every part of his body was Cooked and eaten except the head — bones and guts. He was roasted in the oven (all of his ass), boiled, broiled, fried and stewed. The little boy was next, went the same way. At that time, I was living at 409 E 100 St., near — right side. He told me so often how good Human flesh was I made up my mind to taste it.

On Sunday June the 3rd 1928 I called on you at 406 W 15 St. Brought you pot cheese — strawberries. We had lunch. Grace sat in my lap and kissed me. I made up my mind to eat her.

On the pretense of taking her to a party. You said "Yes," she could go. I took her to an empty house in Westchester I had already picked out. When we got there, I told her to remain outside. She picked wildflowers. I went upstairs and stripped all my clothes off. I knew if I did not I would get her blood on them.

When all was ready I went to the window and called her. Then I hid in a closet until she was in the room. When she saw me all naked she began to cry and tried to run down the stairs. I grabbed her and she said she would tell her mamma.

First I stripped her naked. How she did kick — bite and scratch. I choked her to death, then cut her in small pieces so I could take my meat to my rooms. Cook and eat it. How sweet and tender her little ass was roasted in the oven. It took me nine days to eat her entire body. I did not fuck her though I could of had I wished. She died a virgin."

The letter was clearly from the man who had abducted Grace Budd, since the writer mentioned specific details only he would have known. And the horrific content of the missive gave fresh impetus to the case, with investigators, led by William King, determined to catch the monster who had written it.

Detective King's first action was to inspect the letter closely, comparing the handwriting with the original Western Union telegram that had been sent to the Budds. There was no doubt about it - the handwriting was the same. Then, as he examined the letter and envelope under a magnifying glass he picked up a barely discernable logo – the letters, N.Y.P.C.B.A. Further investigation revealed that it stood for the New York Private Chauffeur's Benevolent Association. The association was glad to open its files to Detective King. However, hours of checking the backgrounds and handwriting of over 400 employees turned up nothing. King wasn't about to give up on the clue, though, he called all of the employees together and appealed for any scrap of information the drivers might have that could help him catch the sadistic child killer.

It paid off. After the session, a man named Lee Sicowski approached King and told him that he had taken some of the association's stationary for private use, and had left some sheets of paper and envelopes in a room that he'd rented. The room was in a cheap boarding house at 200 East 52nd Street.

King hurried to the flophouse, where he interviewed the landlady, Mrs. Frieda Schneider. He could hardly believe his ears when the woman told him that the man who had occupied the room after Sicowski was a close fit for the description of Frank Howard. The man's name, she said, was Albert Fish. Fish had recently checked out, but he received a monthly check from one his sons at the address and always returned to collect it.

William King immediately took a room at the boarding house and waited for Albert Fish to show up.

Three days later, on December 13, 1934, King was called back to the precinct on an urgent matter. He'd barely arrived when there was a call from Mrs. Schneider – Fish was back. King begged her to delay the man as long as she could, then hurried back to the boarding house.

Fish was still there when King arrived. The detective drew his revolver and stepped into the room where his man sat, sipping a cup of tea. His first impression was of a frail, white-haired old man with an untidy mustache and watery blue eyes. Detective King identified himself and asked Fish to accompany him to police headquarters for questioning. Fish nodded in agreement, but as King momentarily dropped his guard, Fish withdrew a razor and slashed at the detective. A short scuffle ensued during which King disarmed and handcuffed the old man.

At the police station, Fish quickly admitted to the abduction and murder of Grace Budd. His intended victim, he explained, had been Edward Budd, who had placed the classified ad. However, when he got to the Budd house and saw Grace, he decided that he wanted her instead. After six years, his recall of the day when he kidnapped Grace was as clear as if it had happened yesterday. It was evident that the fiend had relived it in his mind over and over again.

He said that after he left the Budd's home with Grace, he stopped off to pick up his "instruments of hell," as he called them, a cleaver, saw and butcher's knife. He had left these for safekeeping with a newsagent while he visited the Budd home. He bought a round trip train ticket to Worthington Woods for himself and a one-way ticket for Grace. As they left the train, he recalled, he left his bundle of tools behind and Grace helpfully ran back to retrieve them.

From there Fish took the girl to an abandoned building known as Wisteria Cottage. Leaving the child to play outside, he went up to the second-floor bedroom, where he laid out his bundle of tools, and took off his clothes. Then he called to Grace to come upstairs.

Grace came into the house and up to the bedroom. When she saw the old man naked, she screamed, "I'll tell Momma!" and tried to escape. But Fish grabbed her by the throat and strangled her to death. He was sexually aroused by the act of strangling her. Afterwards, he beheaded and dismembered the body, dissecting her torso at the waist. Parts of her body he took with him wrapped in newspaper, consuming them over the next few days. The rest he left behind until he returned several days later and threw the little girl's remains over a wall at the back of the house.

The story seemed almost too horrific to be true, but when detectives made the trip to Wisteria Cottage themselves, they soon discovered Grace Budd's remains, just as Fish had described them. Neither was this his only murder. Now, seemingly resigned to his fate, he confessed to a string of other homicides that he had committed between 1910 and 1934.

Many of these were proved to be either false or gross exaggerations, but some of them checked out.

One was the murder of Billy Gaffney. On February 11, 1927, four-year-old Billy was playing in the hallway outside his apartment with a three-year-old neighbor also named Billy. A 12-year-old who was babysitting them went inside for only a minute. When he returned both boys were missing. A frantic search eventually turned up the younger child on the top floor of the building. When asked where Billy Gaffney was, the little boy replied: "The boogey man took him."

A massive police search failed to find the four-year-old, and detectives then returned to his playmate and asked him for a description of the "boogeyman" who had taken Billy. The boy said he was a thin old man with gray hair and a gray mustache.

It sounded familiar. A similar description had been given by an eyewitness to a crime committed a few years earlier, the perpetrator of which was known to police as "The Gray Man."

In July 1924, eight-year-old Francis McDonnell was playing on the front porch of his home in Charlton Woods, Staten Island. His mother sitting nearby saw a gaunt old man with gray hair and a gray mustache standing in the road. The man tipped his hat to her and disappeared down the street.

Later that afternoon, the same old man approached some boys playing ball, one of them, Francis McDonnell. The man called Francis over while the other boys continued their game. A few moments later, both Francis and the old man had disappeared. It was only at dinnertime that anyone noticed Francis missing. His father, a policeman, organized a search. They found the boy in the woods under some branches. He had been the victim of a horrendous assault, his clothes ripped away, his suspenders knotted tightly around his neck and his body savagely beaten.

The sheer brutality of these crimes, and the relish with which Fish described them, suggested that he was insane. Dr. Frederic Wertham, who spent more time examining Fish than any other psychiatrist, certainly believed so. To Wertheim, Fish described his many fetishes and perversions, including pushing needles into his scrotum and inserting wool that was doused with lighter fluid into his anus and setting it on fire. He told Wertham how he had carried Grace Budd's ears and nose back to New York with him, wrapped in newspaper, all the while quivering with excitement at the thought of what was inside.

Wertheim later wrote that Fish was "the most polymorphous pervert I had ever known. Someone who practiced every perversion and deviation known to man, from sodomy to sadism, eating excrement and self-mutilation."

But above all, Fish was a sadist of incredible cruelty, a pedophile who, as a self-employed painter, had lurked around basements and cellars for 50 years and preyed upon untold numbers of innocent children. "To the best of my knowledge, Wertham said, "he has raped one hundred children, at least."

Fish's attorney, James Dempsey, followed this line of defense at trial, engaging Dr. Wertham, to testify as to the state of Fish's sanity. Wertham's prepared statement took one hour fifteen minutes to read and concluded with the words, "He is insane."

The jury was unmoved. They took less than an hour to find Fish guilty. He was sentenced to die in the electric chair, the execution scheduled for January 16, 1936.

As his appointment with death grew closer, Fish told reporters that he was looking forward to his execution. "It will be the only thrill I have not tried," he is reported to have said.

Albert Fish died in the electric chair on January 16, 1936, the oldest man ever executed at Sing Sing.

John Wayne Gacy

Killer Clown

"Don't you know clowns can get away with murder?" John Wayne Gacy

Along with Ted Bundy, John Wayne Gacy is arguably the most notorious American serial killer of all time. Like Bundy, Gacy was a man of great promise, a sharp and successful businessman, an outgoing and gregarious individual who hosted elaborate parties for friends and neighbors, a tireless worker for various charities who was photographed with the first lady in recognition of his efforts, a member of the Jolly Jokers organization who dressed up as a clown and entertained children at local hospitals. That was the face John Gacy showed to the world. To his victims, 33 boys and young men aged between 14 and 21, he showed another side – brutal rapist, merciless torturer, cold-blooded killer.

John Wayne Gacy was born in Chicago, Illinois, on March 17, 1942, the second of John Stanley Gacy and Marion Elaine Robinson's three children. As a child, he was overweight and clumsy, but nonetheless active, participating in the Boys' Scouts and holding down various after school jobs. He was close to his two sisters and mother but had a difficult relationship with his alcoholic father, who was often physically abusive toward his wife and children.

Despite this, Gacy seems to have had a relatively happy childhood, albeit one peppered with traumatic experiences. At age nine, he was sexually molested by a friend of his father; at 11, he was struck in the head by a swing, leaving a blood clot that caused him to suffer blackouts; at 17, he was diagnosed with a heart ailment that would cause him problems at various times during his life.

He failed to graduate high school, dropping out to move to Las Vegas where he got a job as a janitor in a funeral parlor. Gacy would only remain here for three months, but one event from this time bears repeating. Gacy later claimed that, on one occasion, he cuddled and caressed the corpse of a young man. The experience sickened him he said, but he also found it exciting.

On returning to Chicago, Gacy enrolled on a business course and thereafter got a job with Nunn-Bush Shoe Company who subsequently transferred him to   Springfield, Illinois as a management trainee. While in Springfield, Gacy became involved in several community organizations, most notably, the Jaycees, eventually becoming first vice-president.

In March 1964, he became engaged to a co-worker named Marlynn Myers. The couple married in September that year. That same year, Gacy had his first homosexual experience. According to Gacy, a colleague of his in the Jaycees plied him with booze and then performed oral sex on him while he was drunk.

Gacy remained in Springfield until 1966, when his father-in-law offered him the chance to run the string of Kentucky Fried Chicken outlets he owned in Waterloo, Iowa. The opportunity was attractive and the Gacys soon relocated to Iowa, where Gacy began learning the business while also becoming involved with the local Jaycees chapter.

Marlynn gave birth to a son, Michael, in March 1967, followed by a daughter named Christine in October 1968. The family moved to a new house in the suburbs. Marlynn was happy being a stay at home mom, while John was enjoying the challenges of running the business and was also planning a campaign for the presidency of the Jaycees. The Gacys seemed to be living the American dream. But already, dark currents were swirling.

Rumors around town had it that John Wayne Gacy was gay and that he continually made passes at the young boys who worked for him at the fast food restaurants. Those close to Gacy put these rumors down to mischief making by his opponents in the Jaycees. In May 1968, they had reason to rethink that assessment when Gacy was arrested for a sexual assault on a 15-year-old named Donald Voorhees. He then made matters worse for himself by hiring another youth to beat up Voorhees in an effort to stop him testifying.

When the matter came to court, Gacy pled guilty to a charge of sodomy and received the maximum penalty, ten years at the Iowa

State Reformatory. Shortly after, Gacy's wife divorced him and gained custody of the children. He would never see any of them again.

While in prison, Gacy was considered a model prisoner, resulting in him being released on June 18, 1970, just 18 months into his 10-year sentence. Gacy returned to his mother's home. His father had died while he was in prison and he deeply regretted that they hadn't reconciled. Despite the abuse Gacy Sr. had meted out during his childhood, John loved him deeply and had been devastated by his death.

Back in Chicago, Gacy got a job as a short-order chef, and with the assistance of his mother, bought a house just outside the Chicago city limits at 8213 West Summerdale Avenue, Norwood Park - an address he'd soon turn into one of the most infamous in America.

On June 1, 1972, Gacy remarried. His new bride was Carole Hoff, a recently divorced mother of two. At around this time, Gacy quit his job as a chef and started a contracting business named PDM Contractors (PDM standing for Painting, Decorating, and Maintenance). As with all of Gacy's business undertakings it was successful almost immediately (by the time he was arrested in 1978, it would be turning over $200 000 a year). But financial success wasn't Gacy's only goal for PDM. He hired mainly teenage boys to work for him and used his position to make homosexual advances towards them.

His neighbors in Norwood Park saw a different Gacy. He was well liked, a generous host who loved hosting dinners and throwing elaborate parties and barbecues. He was also active in his local community, a tireless worker for the Democratic Party and, for three consecutive years, director of Chicago's annual Polish Constitution Day Parade. Through this latter activity, he was introduced to (and photographed with) First Lady Rosalynn Carter on May 6, 1978. Mrs. Carter signed the photo: "To John Gacy. Best wishes. Rosalynn Carter."

Another activity Gacy became involved in was the "Jolly Joker" clown club whose members performed at fundraising events, as well as entertaining hospitalized children. Gacy joined in 1975 and created his own character, "Pogo the Clown." He is known to have performed as Pogo at numerous charitable events.

Also in 1975, Gacy admitted to his wife that he was gay and informed her that their sexual relationship was over. The couple would divorce a year later. By then, Gacy had already begun his murder spree.

The first murder committed by John Wayne Gacy occurred on January 2, 1972, although Gacy would later claim it was accidental. He picked up a 15-year-old youth named Timothy McCoy from Chicago's Greyhound bus terminal. McCoy was en route to Omaha and Gacy offered him a place to stay for the night. The next morning, according to Gacy, the boy entered his bedroom holding a kitchen knife. Convinced that he was about to be attacked, Gacy overpowered the youth and stabbed him to death. Later, when he walked into his kitchen he saw that McCoy had been in the process of preparing breakfast. He'd come into Gacy's room not to attack him, but to call him to the meal. McCoy's became the first corpse consigned to the crawlspace under Gacy's house. There would be others.

Gacy would later state that he experienced an orgasm while stabbing McCoy. "That's when I realized that death was the ultimate thrill," he added.

He repeated the thrill in January 1974. The victim was an unidentified teenage youth who Gacy strangled to death then stored in a closet before burying him in the backyard. Gacy later stated that fluid leaked out of the youth's mouth and nose, staining the carpet. As a result, he began stuffing cloth or paper into his victims' mouths.

In May 1975, Gacy attacked another youth, an employee at PDM, but this time the tables were turned on him. Fifteen-year-old Anthony Antonucci was a member of his school's wrestling team, and when Gacy snapped handcuffs on his wrists, Antonucci got free and wrestled Gacy to the floor, then cuffed Gacy's hands behind his back. Gacy screamed and threatened and eventually Antonucci removed the handcuffs. Antonucci remained in Gacy's employ after the incident, but Gacy never tried anything with him again.

However, one week after the attempted assault on Antonucci, another PDM employee, 17-year-old John Butkovitch, went missing. The day before he disappeared, Butkovitch and Gacy had argued about unpaid wages. Gacy later admitted to luring Butkovitch to his home on the pretense of paying the overdue money. Once there, he overpowered and then strangled the teenager. Gacy was questioned about Butkovitch's disappearance and admitted to having argued with the boy, but insisted he had paid him and sent him on his way.

In April 1976, Gacy abducted and murdered 18-year-old Darrell Sampson. Five weeks later, on May 14, 15-year-old Randall Reffett disappeared while walking home from school; the youth was gagged with a cloth and strangled. Just hours later, Gacy abducted and murdered 14-year-old Samuel Stapleton. Reffett and Stapelton ended up in the same shallow grave in Gacy's crawlspace.

On June 3, 1976, Gacy killed 17-year-old Michael Bonnin, strangling him with a ligature and burying him in the crawl space. Ten days later, 16-year-old William Carroll was murdered and buried directly beneath Gacy's kitchen. Two unidentified youths were killed between June 13 and August 6 and buried in the same grave as Bonnin. They were joined by two more "John Doe" victims, killed between August and October 1976.

On October 24, 1976, Gacy abducted and killed two teenage friends named Kenneth Parker and Michael Marino. Both boys were strangled before being buried in the same grave in the crawl space. Two days later, 19-year-old PDM employee, William Bundy, disappeared. Bundy had told his parents he was going to a party. He ended up in the crawlspace, directly beneath Gacy's master bedroom.

Another PDM employee, 17-year-old Gregory Godzik, went missing in December 1976. Godzik had only worked for PDM for three weeks before his disappeared. He had told his family that

Gacy had him "digging trenches for some kind of drain," in his crawlspace. When Godzik's parents contacted Gacy as to their son's whereabouts, Gacy claimed Greg had told him that he planned on running away from home.

A month later, on January 20, 1977, another PDM employee vanished. John Szyc, 19, was a friend of Butkovich and Godzik. Gacy claimed that Szyc had sold him his Plymouth Satellite because he wanted to raise money to go to California. Szyc's ended up buried in Gacy's crawlspace. Gacy later sold Szyc's car to another PDM employee, Michael Rossi. He also kept Szyc's portable Motorola TV and a class ring, bearing his initials.

Between December 1976 and March 1977, Gacy killed another unidentified victim and also took the life of 20-year-old Jon Prestidge, a Michigan native visiting friends in Chicago. Another unidentified victim followed Prestidge into the crawlspace soon after.

On July 1977, Gacy abducted and killed Matthew Bowman. He was buried in the crawlspace with a tourniquet still knotted around his neck. By the end of the year, another six young men, aged between 16 and 21, had ended up in the space under Gacy's home. The first was 18-year-old Robert Gilroy, last seen alive on September 15. Gilroy was the son of a Chicago Police Sergeant. Ten days later, a 19-year-old U.S. Marine named John Mowery disappeared while walking to his apartment from his mother's home. The next to die was 21-year-old Russell Nelson, who disappeared from a Chicago bar on October 17. Less than four weeks later, 16-year-old Robert Winch was murdered and buried in the crawlspace, and on

November 18, a 20-year-old named Tommy Boling met the same fate.

Three weeks after the murder of Tommy Boling, a 19-year-old U.S. Marine named David Talsma disappeared while on his way to a rock concert in Hammond. Talsma was strangled with a ligature and buried in the crawlspace.

Gacy's next victim, Robert Donnelly, was one of the few who survived his encounter with the killer. Donnelly was abducted at gunpoint on December 30, 1977. He was driven to Gacy's home where he was raped, tortured and sodomized with various objects. His head was held under water in the bathtub until he passed out. Then Gacy revived him, before holding him under water again. Donnelly later testified that he was in so much pain that he begged Gacy to kill him. "I'm getting round to it," was Gacy's reply.

Inexplicably, though, he didn't kill Donnelly. He drove him back to where he'd abducted him and released him. Donnelly reported the assault and Gacy was questioned about it on January 6, 1978. He admitted to having had sex with Donnelly but insisted that everything was consensual. The police believed him and no charges were filed. The following month, Gacy killed a 19-year-old youth named William Kindred. Kindred was the last victim buried in the crawlspace. Gacy was running out of room, the next four corpses would be disposed of in the Des Plaines River.

In March 1978, another victim survived the attentions of John Gacy. The abduction, rape, and torture of 26-year-old Jeffrey Rignall is telling because it offers an insight into Gacy's M.O.

Rignall was lured into Gacy's car with the offer of sharing a joint. Once inside, Gacy pressed a chloroform-soaked rag to his face, then drove Rignall to the house in Norwood Park. Here he was handcuffed, beaten, raped, tortured and sodomized with various objects including dildos and lit candles. Several times he was chloroformed into unconsciousness. Rignall eventually came around in Lincoln Park, amazed that he was alive. He was later informed that he had suffered permanent liver damage, due to the amount of chloroform he had inhaled.

The assault was reported to police and when they failed to act, Rignall took matters into his own hands. All he could remember about the evening was Gacy's black Oldsmobile, and a particular exit on the Kennedy Expressway. Rignall staked out the exit for several weeks until he spotted Gacy's distinctive vehicle. He then tailed the car to Gacy's home at 8213 West Summerdale and passed the information on to police, leading to Gacy's arrest on July 15.

But the arrest did nothing to curtail Gacy's killing spree. While awaiting trial for the Rignall assault he committed four more murders, throwing the bodies from the I-55 Bridge into the Des Plaines River. The first victim disposed of in this way was 20-year-old Timothy O'Rourke, killed in mid-June and found six miles downstream on June 30. Four months later, on November 4, Gacy killed a 19-year-old named Frank Landingin. His body was found on November 12. Three weeks later, 20-year-old James Mazzara disappeared after sharing Thanksgiving dinner with his family; his body was found on December 28.

On December 11, 1978, John Gacy was contracted to do a remodeling job at a Des Plaines pharmacy. While discussing the job with the owner, Phil Torf, Gacy spotted 15-year-old Robert Piest, an employee at the store.

After Gacy left, Piest told his mother that he was going to speak to "some contractor" about a job. When Piest failed to return, his family filed a missing person report with the Des Plaines Police. The owner of the pharmacy told police that Gacy was most probably the contractor Piest had gone to see.

Gacy was questioned but denied offering Piest a job, or even talking to the boy. When questioned as to why he had returned to the pharmacy at 8 p.m. on the day Piest had disappeared, Gacy said Phil Torf had called him to tell him he'd left his appointment book behind. But Torf denied having made the call, which immediately raised suspicions.

Des Plaines police began checking into Gacy's background and discovered that he had an outstanding battery charge against him in Chicago and had served time in Iowa for sodomy. And a search of Gacy's house, on December 13, increased their suspicions even further. Among the items found were: a 1975 high school class ring engraved with the initials J.A.S., various driver's licenses, handcuffs, a two-by-four with holes drilled in the ends, a syringe, clothing which was much too small for Gacy, a 6mm starter pistol and a photo receipt from the pharmacy where Robert Piest had worked. Still, it wasn't enough to arrest Gacy, so the police put him under surveillance instead, assigning two two-man teams to the task.

Slowly, the evidence against Gacy began to build. First, Michael Rossi informed investigators about Gregory Godzik's disappearance. Then Gacy's former wife informed them about the disappearance of John Butkovich. The same day, the high school class ring was traced to a John A. Szyc, also missing. Szyc's mother informed police about her son's Plymouth Satellite which he'd apparently sold to Gacy prior to his disappearance.

Not that any of this seemed to bother Gacy. He had become quite friendly with the detectives following him, inviting them to join him for meals in various restaurants and for drinks in his home. He seemed to be turning the whole thing into a game, constantly trying to lose his tail (and succeeding on a number of occasions), flouting the traffic laws, knowing that the officers wouldn't arrest him on any trivial charge.

On December 17, investigators carried out a test on Gacy's Oldsmobile using three search-and-rescue dogs. They wanted to see if Robert Piest had ever been in Gacy's vehicle, but as soon as one of the dogs got in, he lay down on the passenger seat, in a "death reaction," indicating that Piest had been in the vehicle, but it had been after he was killed.

By this time, Gacy was beginning to crack. He was unkempt, unshaven, and bleary eyed. He was also drinking heavily and appeared anxious. On the evening of December 20, he drove to his lawyers' office to discuss a civil suit aimed at ending the police surveillance. He was drunk but immediately asked for whiskey. When lawyer, Sam Amirante, returned with a bottle, Gacy picked up the Daily Herald newspaper that was lying on Amirante's desk.

He pointed to an article about the disappearance of Robert Piest and told the lawyer, "This boy is dead. He's in the river."

Over the next several hours, Gacy gave a rambling confession to his lawyers, starting by informing them that he'd been "judge, jury and executioner of many, many people." He told them about the bodies buried under the crawlspace in his house, dismissing most of them as "hustlers" and "liars" who he had given his "rope trick." At one point during the confession, Gacy fell asleep and Amirante phoned to arrange a psychiatric appointment for Gacy that morning. However, when he awoke, Gacy said that he couldn't attend the consultation. Amazingly, he acted as though nothing had happened, and left, saying he had things to do in his business.

After leaving the lawyer's office, Gacy drove to a gas station where he handed a bag of marijuana to the attendant. The youth immediately passed the bag to the surveillance officers, informing them that Gacy had told him: "The end is coming. These guys are going to kill me." Gacy then visited his friend Ronald Rhode, who he told, "I killed thirty people, give or take a few." He then drove to the home of his former employees Michael Rossi and David Cram and asked them to drive him to his father's grave at Maryhill Cemetery.

As Gacy drove to various locations that morning, police became concerned that he might be intending to cheat justice by committing suicide. They therefore pulled him over and arrested him for possession and distribution of marijuana.

That same afternoon, the search warrant was issued for Gacy's home. Crime scene investigators entering the house immediately commented on the smell of decomposition. They soon found its source. As evidence technician Daniel Genty began digging in the southwest corner of the crawlspace, he uncovered putrefied flesh just inches below the surface. Soon after, he found a human arm bone.

Confronted with the discovery, Gacy told officers that he wanted to "clear the air." He began making his confession in the early hours of December 22, 1978, claiming that, since 1972, he had killed approximately 25 to 30 young men. He said that he either forced the victims into his car or conned them by producing a badge and pretending to be a police officer. Back at his house, the victims would be handcuffed, then choked with a rope or a board as they were being sexually assaulted. Gacy would often stick clothing in the victims' mouths to muffle their screams. Most of his victims were strangled with a tourniquet, sometimes convulsing on the floor for an "hour or two," before they died. Asked about the two-by-four to which he had manacled many of his victims, Gacy said he had been inspired by the murders committed by Dean Corll, in Houston.

Twenty-nine bodies were eventually recovered from Gacy's house and a further four corpses found in the Des Plaines River were also attributed to him.

John Wayne Gacy went on trial for the murders on February 6, 1980. Five weeks later, on March 12, the jury deliberated for just two hours before returning a guilty verdict. Gacy was sentenced to death on each of the 12 counts of murder for which the prosecution had sought the death penalty, with the date of execution set for June 2, 1980.

However, as in all capital cases, there were appeals to work through. Gacy would remain on death row for 14 years before his execution date eventually came around.

On the morning of May 9, 1994, Gacy was transferred from the Menard Correctional Center in Chester, Illinois to Stateville Correctional Center in Crest Hill. That afternoon, he was allowed a private picnic on the prison grounds with his family. That evening, he was visited by a Catholic priest before he was escorted to the death cell.

The execution did not go as smoothly as expected due to clogging of the IV tube administering the lethal chemicals into Gacy's arm. After a delay of 18 minutes, Gacy was pronounced dead at 12:58 a.m. on May 10, 1994.

His final words were reported to be, "Kiss my ass."

Randy Kraft

The Scorecard Killer

In the early hours of May 14, 1983, two California Highway
Patrolmen pulled over a suspected drunk driver on the San Diego
Freeway, near Mission Viejo. The driver staggered from his
vehicle, discarding a beer bottle as he did. He insisted he was
sober, although a field sobriety test proved otherwise. The officers
then placed the man, identified as 38-year-old Randy Steven Kraft,
of Long Beach, under arrest for driving under the influence.

It looked like a routine DUI, but as Sgt. Michael Howard
approached Kraft's Toyota Celica, he saw another man slumped
over in the passenger's seat. The man's pants were unzipped, his
genitals exposed. Howard rapped on the window and got no
response. He then opened the car door and tried to rouse the man
by shaking him – nothing. Howard placed his fingers to the man's
throat and detected no pulse. He did, however, notice red marks
on the man's neck, a clear sign of strangulation.

A murder suspect now, Kraft was taken into custody. But the evening's gruesome discoveries were not done yet. Among the discarded beer bottles, the supply of prescription painkillers and the dried blood in Kraft's vehicle, police discovered a stash of macabre Polaroids, showing 47 nude young men, all of whom appeared to be either dead or unconscious. And in the trunk, they found a clue as to what they were dealing with - a notepad with 61 perplexing entries, that detectives soon realized was a list of murder victims.

Already reeling from the recent arrests of "Trash Bag Killer" Patrick Kearney and "Freeway Killer" William Bonin, California had another serial killer on its hands. And, if the numbers were correct, Randy Kraft had claimed more victims than Kearney and Bonin combined.

Randy Kraft was born on March 19, 1945, in Long Beach, California, the youngest child, and only son, of Harold and Opal Kraft, Wyoming natives who had moved west just the year before. In 1948, the family moved to Midway City, in Orange County. The community was conservative and the young Randy seems to have absorbed this attitude into his own worldview. His high school classmates remember him as being ultra right wing, and he carried these views with him into his first year of college. He was, for example, a vocal supporter of the Vietnam War, and a tireless campaigner for conservative presidential candidate Barry Goldwater, in 1964.

The following year, though, brought a radical change to the straight-laced Randy. He grew his hair, cultivated a mustache and got a part-time job as a barman in a gay bar. Rumors started to circulate around campus of his fondness for bondage and he began consuming copious amounts of Valium (to ward off headaches caused by a childhood fall, he said).

In 1966, he moved off campus and set up house with a male friend in Huntington Beach. He also began to spend all of his free time in gay bars, and acquired his first arrest – for lewd conduct – after propositioning an undercover police officer.

Despite a less that diligent application to his studies, Kraft graduated in 1968 with a bachelor's degree in economics. Soon after, he immersed himself in another political campaign, working so diligently for Robert Kennedy that he received a personal letter of thanks from the senator. He was devastated when Kennedy was assassinated. Just days later, he joined the U.S. Air Force and was posted to Edwards Air Force Base, where he would eventually supervise the painting of test planes.

A year later, in 1969, Kraft stunned his family by telling them he was gay. Then, after his discharge from the military on "medical grounds," he resumed his bartending career, and fully embraced the gay lifestyle. "There's a part of me that you will never know," Kraft told friends who were perplexed by the change in him. A part that was, no doubt, already fantasizing about killing. Soon he would start turning those fantasies into reality.

On October 5, 1971, police found a decomposing corpse alongside the Ortega Highway, in Orange County. The body turned out to be that of Wayne Joseph Dukette, a 30-year-old bartender at the Stables gay bar in Long Beach, who had been reported missing two

weeks earlier. The coroner fixed his date of death at around
September 20, but found nothing to indicate foul play. He was
wrong. Wayne Dukette was Randy Kraft's first victim. The entry
"STABLE" on Kraft's scorecard is believed to refer to Dukette.

Fifteen months later, on December 26, 1972, a motorist traveling
the 405 Freeway near Seal Beach, spotted a nude body lying at the
side of the road. The motorist alerted the police, who discovered
the corpse of Edward Daniel Moore, a 20-year-old Marine based at
Camp Pendleton. Moore had left the barracks on Christmas Eve.
He'd been strangled, bludgeoned and apparently tossed from a
moving car. There were clear signs of torture on the body,
including bite marks on the genitals. A sock had been jammed up
the victim's rectum.

The next body was discovered beside the Terminal Island
Freeway, on February 6, 1973. The victim, who has never been
identified, was estimated to be in his late teens or early twenties.
And police had the first indications of a pattern. As in the murder
of Edward Moore, a sock had been forced into the man's anus.

If this was a series, the killer was escalating. On Easter Sunday,
police made another grim discovery, this time in Huntington
Beach. The corpse was fully dressed, although barefooted.
Underneath his bloody slacks, his genitals had been hacked away.
Ligature marks on his wrists suggested that the injury may have
been inflicted prior to death.

The mutilation of the next victim was even more severe. In fact,
the corpse was dismembered and scattered across two counties:

the head found in Long Beach; the torso, right leg and both arms in San Pedro; the left leg in Sunset Beach. There were rope marks on the wrists and evidence that the corpse had been refrigerated prior to disposal.

And still, the death toll kept mounting. Ron Wiebe, a 20-year-old from Fullerton, vanished on July 28, 1973. He was found next to the 405 Freeway in Seal Beach, beaten and strangled, with bite marks on his stomach and penis and a sock shoved into his rectum.

Then, 23-year-old art student Vincent Cruz Mestas was found in a ravine in the San Bernardino Mountains on December 29, 1973. His hands were missing, and plastic sandwich bags covered the bloody stumps. A pencil had been forced into his penis prior to death.

Six months later, 20-year-old Malcolm Eugene Little was found propped up against a mesquite tree beside Highway 86, in Imperial County. His genitals had been severed and a tree branch had been rammed six inches into his rectum.

Another U.S. Marine fell prey to the killer three weeks later. Roger Dickerson, 18, was found near a golf club in Laguna Beach. He'd been strangled and sodomized and there were bite marks on his genitals.

August brought two more gruesome discoveries, 25-year-old Thomas Paxton Lee, known around Long Beach as a gay street hustler, and, 23-year-old Gary Wayne Cordova. Neither victim had been mutilated and the murders were not initially connected to the unknown killer.

There was little doubt about the next discovery, though. James Dale Reeves was found in Irvine on November 29, 1974. The killer posed the body with legs spread, a tree limb four feet long and three inches in diameter protruding from the anus.

In December 1974, John Leras, a 17-year-old high school student, was found floating in the surf at Sunset Beach, a wooden surveyor's stake hammered into his rectum. Leras had been strangled while bound. Two sets of footprints leading from the car park to the water seemed to indicate that two killers had been involved.

Three weeks later, on January 17, 1975, construction workers found 21-year-old Craig Victor Jonaites strangled to death alongside the Pacific Coast Highway, near Long Beach. He had not been mutilated, but the presence of alcohol and Valium in his blood suggested that he might have fallen prey to the same killer.

By now, there'd been fourteen brutal murders of young men in a little over three years and yet the police had nothing. Not only that, but the killer appeared to be accelerating. Something had to be done to stop him.

On January 24, 1975, a week after the discovery of the latest victim, detectives from several jurisdictions met in Santa Ana, to organize a task force. Also present was a profiler from the FBI's Behavioral Science Unit, a special investigator from the California

State Attorney General's office and several forensic psychologists. Yet a re-examination of the various crimes turned up no significant leads. The killer was clever, careful and resourceful – and he was still killing.

On March 29, 1975, friends of 19-year-old Keith Daven Crotwell, saw him hitch a ride with a black-and-white Mustang in Long Beach. Crotwell was not seen again until May 8, when three boys found his severed head near the Long Beach Marina. Police traced the registration of the Mustang and questioned its owner, Randy Kraft, on May 19. Kraft admitted giving Crotwell a ride, but said he had dropped him off at an all-night café. With no evidence to suggest otherwise, the police were forced to release him without charge.

The interrogation by police might have unsettled Kraft, because he took a 24-week break before he killed again. Larry Gene Walters, 21, was murdered in Los Angeles County on Halloween, 1975. Two months later, 22-year-old Mark Hall disappeared from a New Year's Eve party, in San Juan Capistrano. His nude corpse was found on January 3, 1976, in the Cleveland National Forest. He'd been sodomized and tortured prior to death: his legs slashed with a broken bottle; his eyes, face, chest and genitals burned with a cigarette lighter; a cocktail swizzle stick jammed through his penis into his bladder; his genitals severed and stuffed into his rectum. The medical examiner was able to deduce that the victim had been alive throughout much of the ordeal.

At around this time, Randy Kraft split with his long-time lover Jeff Graves and moved into a Laguna Beach apartment with 19-year-old Jeff Seelig. And police were suddenly confronted with a new

spate of murders, nine slayings confirmed in 1976, all of them
teenagers, their bodies dismembered and discarded beside
highways and in dumpsters. The task team was baffled. Was this a
different killer, or had the man they'd been seeking changed his
M.O. and victim type?

Further complicating matters was the arrest of "Trashbag Killer"
Patrick Kearney in 1977. At first, authorities thought Kearney
responsible for Kraft's murders, even though their M.O.'s were
significantly different. Kearney's victims were all shot in the head,
and he seemed offended by suggestions that he had used torture.

In fact, Kraft, secure in his new relationship with Jeff Seelig, had
taken a break from murder. Seelig would later tell investigators
that although he and Kraft regularly picked up hitchhikers for
threesomes, he had never seen Kraft display   any tendency
towards violence.

Whether that is true or not, the beast inside Randy Kraft emerged
again on April 16, 1978, when he picked up 19-year-old Marine,
Scott Michael Hughes. Hughes was found the following day beside
the 91 Freeway in Orange County. He'd been strangled to death,
his genitals mutilated with a knife, one of his testicles removed.

Two months later, 23-year-old Roland Young was found stabbed
to death, his genitals mutilated. Young had just been released from
the Orange County jail on a charge of public intoxication. A week
after the murder of Roland Young, Kraft murdered another Marine.
Twenty-three-year-old Richard Keith was hiking back to Camp

Pendleton when he crossed paths with the killer. His body was found by an off-duty fireman the next day.

The next victim was Keith Klingbeil, found by a motorist on the 1-5 near Mission Viejo on July 6, 1978. Klingbeil was still alive, but died at the scene while paramedics fought to save his life. Then, Michael Joseph Inderbeiten, a 21-year-old Long Beach truck driver, was found, emasculated and sodomized, his eyelids seared with an automobile cigarette lighter.

On June 16, 1979, motorists traveling the 405 Freeway in Irvine were stunned to see a man pushed from a moving vehicle. He was another young Marine, Donald Harold Crisel and there were ligature marks on his neck and wrists. Death, though, was from an overdose of booze and painkillers.

As the body count continued to spiral, gay bars throughout southern California began posting warnings for their customers. It did nothing to stop the slaughter, over a dozen male corpses, ranging in age from 13 to 24, were found littering the freeways in 1979.

Neither was Randy Kraft confining his activities to California anymore. As a freelance data-processing consultant, he traveled extensively during this period, taking in Michigan, Oregon, New York and Florida. He also traveled to Mexico, and spent time in San Diego and Lake Tahoe. And wherever he went corpses seemed to turn up.

Michael Sean O'Fallon, a 17-year-old Colorado native, was killed in
Oregon in 1980, his murder bearing all the hallmarks of Kraft's
work. Then, on September 3, 1980, children playing near El Toro
Marine Airbase found the corpse of 19-year-old U.S. Marine,
Robert Loggins. Another victim, Michael Duane Cluck, 17, was
killed in April 1981, while hitchhiking from California to Oregon.

On July 29, 1981, residents of Echo Park, in Los Angeles,
complained to police about a rank odor coming from the nearby
Hollywood Freeway. Officers investigated and found two corpses.
Thirteen-year-old Raymond Davis had disappeared while
searching for a lost dog, 16-year-old Robert Avila, had gone
missing from Hollywood weeks before. Three weeks later, 17-
year-old Christopher Williams was found dead beside a road in the
San Bernardino Mountains.

1982 brought more murders, 26-year-old Brian Whitcher, along
the I-5 near Portland on November 26, Dennis Alt and Chris
Schoenborn in Grand Rapids, Michigan, on December 7, while
Kraft was in town for a computer conference. Their corpses were
found together in Plainfield Township two days later, both doped
with booze and Valium, then strangled. Schoenborn had a
ballpoint pen from Kraft's hotel thrust into his bladder through his
penis. Kraft gave the murders the designation "GR2" on his
scorecard.

Two more men turned up in Oregon in December, but by now
police had picked up on the similarities in the Oregon and
California murders. They requested airline passenger records for
the L.A. to Portland route - Randy Kraft's name appeared 18 times.

Before they could follow up the lead, though, Kraft had been arrested with the corpse in his passenger seat.

The killer was in custody, now began the job of ensuring that he would never be free to kill again, and the starting point for prosecutors was the list, the "scorecard," that had been found in Kraft's car.

This consisted of two neatly printed columns, 30 items on the left side, 31 on the right. It began with "STABLE" and ended with "WHAT YOU GOT." In between were clues like, "2 IN 1 HITCH," "GR2," "PORTLAND BLOOD," and "JAIL OUT." Some were obvious references to specific murders, others more difficult to decipher. Whatever their meaning, it seemed clear that at least 61 incidents were being referenced in a unique and macabre scorecard, documenting Randy Kraft's decade-long career as a sadistic serial murderer.

Kraft wasn't talking, though, he insisted that the list was entirely innocent, a catalog of sexual encounters with gay lovers. However, his Polaroid collection, showing many of the murder victims in poses that suggested they were already dead, was more difficult to explain.

More than five years after his arrest, Kraft's much-delayed trial finally came to court on September 26, 1988. Thirteen months and $10 million later, it concluded with a guilty verdict on 16 charges of capital murder. On August 11, 1989, the jury recommended the death penalty and Judge McCartin made it official on November 29, sentencing Kraft to die in California's gas chamber.

As at time of writing, Randy Kraft awaits his execution on death row at San Quentin State Prison.

Dennis Rader

The BTK Killer

"The code word for me will be....Bind them, torture them, kill them, B.T.K." – Dennis Rader

Wichita, a city that sits astride the Arkansas River in south-central Kansas, is renowned for its entrepreneurial spirit with Pizza Hut, White Castle, Taco Tico and the Coleman Corporation all having their roots here. It is also the place where the electric guitar was invented and is a major center for the U.S. aeronautics industry.

But for a period of thirty years, from 1974 to 2005, the "Air Capital of the World," had a rather more sinister claim to fame. It was home to one of the most brutal and elusive serial killers in U.S. history – The BTK killer.

Over a 17-year period from 1974 to 1991, BTK (standing for Bind, Torture, Kill) took ten victims, ranging in age from 9 to 62. He'd break into their houses and wait for them to come home. Then he'd threaten them with a gun, bind and torture them and finally dispatch them by strangulation.

Then, in 1991, after the murder of 62-year-old Dolores Davis, the killings suddenly stopped. Police speculated that BTK had been incarcerated for some other crime or had died. They were wrong. The killer reappeared in 2004, not to kill this time, merely to taunt the police and boast about his crimes. That the notes and parcels came from the killer was not in doubt – he knew details of the crime scenes that had never been released to the public, and he included in the packages, souvenirs, and photographs to back up his claims.

Ultimately though, his arrogance and need for attention would prove his downfall, and when he was arrested, the people of Wichita would be stunned to learn his identity.

The first of the BTK killings occurred on January 15, 1974. On that chilly day, 15-year-old Charlie Otero arrived home from school to the suburban home he shared with his parents and four siblings.

As he opened the front door he noticed that the house seemed unusually quiet. It unnerved him, something seemed wrong. "Mom? Dad?" he called. No reply. With a feeling of unease welling up inside him, Charlie walked toward his parents' bedroom. Here, he discovered his father, Joseph, lying face down on the floor. His mother, Julie, lay on the bed, like Joseph Otero, she was bound, hand and foot. She'd also been gagged. Both of them were obviously dead and, for a moment, Charlie was rooted to the spot in shock. Then he ran from the house and alerted a neighbor who called the police.

As police searched the house it soon became clear that what Charlie had seen was just a foretaste of the horror. Mercifully, he'd been spared finding his 9-year-old brother, Joseph Jr., strangled in his room, or his 11-year-old sister, Josephine, hanging by her neck from a pipe in the basement.

Investigators began putting the pieces of the brutal multiple murder together. It appeared that the killer had a good understanding of the Otero family's routine. He'd waited until Joseph Otero left the house to take his three older children to school. Then he'd somehow talked his way into the residence and subdued Mrs. Otero and the two younger children. He'd cut the telephone wire and waited for Joseph Otero to return. Then, probably using a gun and threats against his family, the killer had subdued and bound Joseph Otero.

Given the execution-style nature of the killings, investigators looked into Joseph Otero's background. He was an airforce veteran and a former boxer who was also trained in judo. His wife, too, was an experienced judoka. And yet, they didn't seem to have put up a struggle. It all pointed to a meticulously planned and executed attack.

But not a revenge killing as detectives had first assumed. And not a robbery either – nothing of value had been taken from the house. No, the semen stains found in various locations pointed to a sexual deviant. One who hadn't sexually assaulted the victims, but had masturbated over their bodies. There was something else too, something police were reluctant to make public. "The way in which family members were slain indicates a fetish on the part of the assailant," was all a spokesman would admit. Later, it would emerge that Julie and Josephine Otero had both been tortured prior to death.

Three months later, on April 4, 1974, BTK struck again (although this crime would only be linked to him after he confessed). When 20-year-old Kathryn Bright arrived home at 1 p.m. there was an intruder waiting in her house. The intruder seemed not to have counted on the presence of Kathryn's 19-year-old brother, Kevin, but he adapted quickly, first demanding money, then forcing Kevin to tie his sister to a chair. The man then took Kevin to another room, tied and gagged him and then tried to strangle him. When Kevin struggled, the man shot him twice in the head. Assuming he was dead, the assailant went back to the other room where, after a time, Kevin could hear sounds of distress from his sister. Despite, his injuries he managed to stagger from the house and get help. By the time police got to the house, though, the assailant was gone. They discovered Kathryn with three deep wounds to her abdomen. She died in hospital 5 hours later.

In October 1974, Don Granger, a reporter with the Wichita Eagle received a call from a man claiming to be the killer of the Otero family. The man told Granger to go to the Wichita Public Library and look inside a particular mechanical engineering textbook. Granger did as directed and found a letter claiming responsibility for the Otero murders, and promising more to come. The author of the letter authenticated his claims by including details not available to the general public. He had made some half-hearted attempts to appear semi-literate with deliberate misspellings and grammatical errors, but he used words like "psychotic," "complicated," and "perversion" spelled correctly and used in context. He also recommended a nickname for himself, stating; "The code word for me will be....Bind them, torture them, kill them, B.T.K."

After that, the BTK killer dropped from sight. There were no further letters and no killings until March 17, 1977. On that date, Wichita police were dispatched to a home on South Hydraulic Street. They found 26-year-old Shirley Vian lying partially dressed on her bed, hands and feet bound, a plastic bag pulled over her head. She'd been strangled with a length of cord that matched those used in the Otero homicides. The killer had locked Mrs. Vian's three young children in a closet. They'd escaped and alerted neighbors who'd called the police.

As in the case of the Otero murders, the crime appeared to have been carefully planned and executed. There was strong evidence that the killer had kept Shirley Vian under surveillance for some time. One of her sons said he'd been approached on the street that morning, shown his mother's photograph and asked for directions to their home.

On December 8, 1977, BTK placed a 911 call and told the dispatcher "Go to this address. You will find a homicide - Nancy Fox." Officers raced to the scene and found 25-year-old Nancy Jo Fox strangled to death with a nylon stocking. Unlike previous victims, she was fully clothed, but police found semen at the scene. An autopsy would later reveal that the victim had not been sexually assaulted.

Then, as abruptly as they'd started, the killings stopped. As in 1974, it appeared that BTK was either sated or had disappeared. He hadn't though, and he wanted the police and public to know it. On January 31, 1978, he sent a letter, containing a short poem about Shirley Vian, to the Wichita Eagle. When that letter didn't garner the publicity he wanted, he sent a letter to a local television station. "How many do I have to kill," he asked, "before I get my name in the paper or some national attention?"

In this latest letter, BTK claimed seven victims (the 7th being Kathryn Bright) and blamed the murders on "a demon" that lived inside him. He also compared his crimes to Jack the Ripper, Son of Sam, and the Hillside Strangler.

On April 28, 1979, BTK waited inside the house of the latest victim he'd chosen, a 63-year-old woman. When the householder didn't show, he became impatient and left, leaving behind a note; "Be glad you weren't here, because I was."

Then he dropped from sight again. Few serial killers have as long a cooling off period as BTK. For the first half of the eighties, he lay dormant, neither committing any crimes nor communicating with the police. The BTK investigation, though, continued. In 1983, two teams of detectives took on the massive task of obtaining blood samples from 200 suspects, spread across the country. In 1984, a task team, dubbed "The Ghostbusters," reworked the evidence with the aid of a computer expert.

As the crimes had all occurred within a 3 ½ mile radius, investigators believed they were looking for a local man and began to compile lists of every white male living within a quarter-mile of each of the crime scenes. They also put together a list of white male students who had attended Wichita State University between 1974 and 1979 (one of the BTK letters had been traced to a copier at the university).

Another key piece of evidence was the semen left at the various crime scenes, which was of a type present in only 6 percent of males according to lab technicians.

All of this information was checked and collated by computer, giving investigators a concise list of 225 suspects. Yet despite over 100,000 man-hours invested in the case, none of them checked out. BTK continued to lay low and eventually the search for him was scaled down to a single detective, Lt. Kenneth Landwehr.

Then, in 1985, BTK reappeared. On April 27 of that year, 53-year-old Marine Hedge was abducted from her home on Independence Street, Park City. She was found eight days later on a rural dirt road. She'd been strangled with a pair of pantyhose. After an 18 month hiatus, the killer struck again, strangling 28-year- old Vicki Wegerle to death in her home on September 16, 1986. Wegerle was the mother of two children, one of whom was in the house at the time of the murder.

BTK's last victim was Delores Davis, 63, killed almost 5 years later on January 19, 1991. Once again, BTK disappeared and the people of Wichita hoped that they had seen the last of him.

Over a decade passed, with no further murders, no communication
from the killer. Then, on March 19, 2004, BTK returned to
terrorize the long-suffering citizens of Wichita. In a letter to the
Wichita Eagle, he claimed responsibility for the 1986 murder of
Vicki Wegerle, provided crime scene photographs and Wegerle's
driver's license to authenticate his story.

Ken Landwehr, still working the BTK case after more than 20
years, confirmed that the letter was from BTK, and when The
Eagle ran the story, it triggered mass panic in the city. Sales of
security systems, guns, personal alarms, pepper spray and other
security devices went through the roof, people traveled in pairs
and entered their homes with weapons drawn. The case garnered
national and international media coverage. CNN, MSNBC and Good
Morning America ran features. The questions that everyone
wanted answered were; Would he kill again, and would the police
get him this time?

But BTK seemed less interested in killing and more interested in
garnering attention for himself. A deluge of correspondence
followed. In May, a word puzzle was received by TV station KAKE.
Then, on June 9, a package was found taped to a stop sign at the
corner of First and Kansas. It contained graphic descriptions of the
Otero murders and a sketch labeled 'The Sexual Thrill Is My Bill."
In October 2004, a manila envelope was dropped into a UPS box in
Wichita containing a series of cards with bondage imagery and a
threat to the life of lead investigator Ken Landwehr. There was
also a list of clues to the killer's identity, most of which turned out
to be false.

Another package surfaced in December 2004. This one contained Nancy Fox's driver's license and a plastic doll, bound hand and foot with a plastic bag pulled over its head.

In one of his letters, Rader asked police if a floppy disk could be traced or not. The police answered this question via an ad posted in the Wichita Eagle saying (falsely) that it could not. On February 16, 2005, TV station KSAS received an envelope that included a Memorex floppy disk. Embedded in the metadata of a deleted Microsoft Word document they found the name, "Christ Lutheran Church." The document was marked as last modified by "Dennis." A search of the church's website showed the name Dennis Rader, president of the congregation council. Police immediately put Rader under surveillance.

Meanwhile, investigators obtained a warrant for the medical records of Rader's daughter and tested a tissue sample against DNA evidence found at the BTK crime scenes. They got a match.

Rader was arrested while driving near his home on February 25, 2005. Immediately after his arrest, officers searched his home, the church he attended, and his office at City Hall. Asked if he knew why he was being arrested, Rader responded; "Oh, I have my suspicions."

He'd later explain that he chose to resurface in 2004 because of a feature on Court TV about the case, and the release of a book, Nightmare in Wichita: The Hunt for the BTK Strangler by Robert Beattie. He said he wanted to tell his own story. He also said he was bored because his children had grown up and he had too much time on his hands.

On February 28, 2005, Rader was formally charged with the BTK murders.

Because his crimes were committed during a period when the death penalty was suspended in Kansas, that option was never open to prosecutors. Still, they were determined that Rader would spend the rest of his life behind bars.

The trial was set down for June 27, but ahead of that date, Rader changed his plea to guilty. He was sentenced to 10 consecutive life terms, meaning he would have to serve a minimum of 175 years before being eligible for parole.

Dennis Rader is currently imprisoned at the El Dorado Correctional Facility, held in solitary confinement for his own protection.

Richard Ramirez

The Night Stalker

"Dying doesn't scare me, I'll be in hell. With Satan." – Richard Ramirez

For a thirteen-month period, from June 1985 to August 1986, the residents of Los Angeles County lived in terror of a vicious murderer, the mysterious "Night Stalker."

The phantom came in the night, sneaking into his victims' bedrooms as they slept, dispatching any male occupants with a gunshot to the head, then playing out his sick fantasies on the female, raping and degrading and brutalizing the unfortunate woman. Often he'd then murder the victim. However, despite the viciousness of his attacks, some survived, while he inexplicably chose to spare others.

The killer would eventually be apprehended and identified as Ricardo Leyva Ramirez a.k.a. Richard Ramirez, a high school dropout and professed Satanist.

Ramirez had moved to L.A. in 1978. Before that, he was a resident of his hometown of El Paso, Texas, the youngest child in a family of three boys and two girls. His father, according to neighbors, had a temper and would sometimes beat the boy. To escape, Ramirez would hang out in a local cemetery, sometimes even spending the night. This may have fuelled his initial attraction to the macabre.

Ramirez suffered epileptic seizures as a child, and was a loner in school, often ridiculed for his thin and girlish appearance. Despite this, he often insisted to people that he would one day be famous.

At the age of 13, Ramirez fell under the influence of his cousin, Mike, a veteran who had served with the Green Berets in Vietnam. Mike become somewhat of a father substitute to Ramirez and impressed the young boy with tales of torturing and mutilating Vietcong prisoners. Mike boasted about raping and murdering women in Vietnam. He even had Polaroids to prove it and proudly showed these to Richard while they were hanging out and getting high. It was on one of these occasions that Mike's wife began to nag him about getting a job. The vet pulled a gun and shot her in the face, killing her instantly, spattering Ramirez with blood.

Mike was arrested and found guilty, but the judge took into account the effect of his horrible war experiences and the sentence was lenient.

It was around this time that Richard's family began to notice changes in his behavior. He began skipping school and spending all of his time smoking marijuana. To support his drug use, he began stealing.

Ramirez dropped out of school in the ninth grade and soon thereafter ensconced for L.A. where he fell into a life of idleness and criminality. His days were spent getting high and eating junk food (a habit that caused his teeth to rot and gave him foul smelling breath). By night he was committing burglary and petty theft, resulting in two arrests, in Pasadena in 1981 and Los Angeles in 1984.

Little is known of the first few years that Ramirez spent in L.A. Given subsequent events, and what we know of typical serial killer behavior, it is safe to assume that while he was becoming more experienced as a burglar, his fantasy life was also evolving.

Perhaps he started taking greater risks, enjoying the thrill of standing in his victims' bedrooms while they slept, enjoying the feeling of power he had over them, no doubt wondering what it would be like to escalate things to the next level, as his hero, Mike, had done. Maybe he started stealing items, not just for their value, but as souvenirs that he could hold later as he re-imagined his crimes. Without doubt, these fantasies would have escalated, until the mere imagining was no longer enough. Until he felt compelled to act on the horror movie that was running in a continuous loop within his mind.

And so it was that, on June 28, 1984, Richard Ramirez, arrived at the Glassel Park home of 79-year-old, Jennie Vincow. The elderly woman had left a window open because of the heat of the evening. Ramirez removed the screen and climbed in.

The victim's son discovered her body the next day. She had been stabbed repeatedly, and her throat was slashed so savagely that she was almost decapitated. The autopsy revealed signs of sexual assault.

In recounting his first crime, the serial killer, Ted Bundy, recalled that he felt disgusted with what he had done. Ramirez may have experienced similar emotional turmoil – at first. Then he likely revisited the crime in his mind, reliving the rape and murder over and over again. He may have told himself that he'd never do it again, may even have tried to control his urges. But as the remembrance faded, the need to replenish it would have been nigh on impossible to resist.

The Night Stalker had lain dormant for eight months. He was ready to kill again.

On March 17, 1985, 20-year-old Angela Barrios was attacked when returning to her condo in Rosemead, a town northeast of Los Angeles. The attacker threatened her with a gun and then fired point blank at her head. Miraculously, the bullet was deflected by her car keys as she raised her hands to protect herself. She fell to the floor and played dead as the attacker stepped over her and entered the condo.

Angela wasn't sure how long she lay there, fearing for her life. After a while, she staggered to her feet and ran from the garage just as the man reappeared. She heard another shot fired and was sure that this time, he'd finish her off. But as quickly as the attacker had appeared, he vanished, leaving Angela hardly able to believe that she'd survived.

She hurried back to the condo to call the police, and there made a gruesome discovery. Her roommate, Dayle Okazaki, was lying face down on the kitchen floor in a pool of her own blood. Angela rushed to the phone and dialed 911.

Yet even as the police rushed to the scene, Ramirez was committing another murder. Perhaps frustrated by Angela's escape, he traveled to nearby Monterey Park and found another victim, shooting 30-year-old Tsia-Lian Yu to death on a sidewalk.

After his first kill, Ramirez had been inactive for eight months, this time, he waited just three days before he struck again, raping and murdering an eight-year-old girl in Eagle Rock, California.

On March 27, 1984, he committed another double homicide, killing Vincent Zazzara and his wife Maxine. Mr. Zazzara was killed by a bullet wound to the temple; his wife was severely and sickeningly mutilated, stabbed repeatedly around the face, neck, abdomen, and groin. Her eyes had been gouged out. Ramirez had also ransacked the house, removing various valuables.

The Zazzara homicides are significant in that they mark the first time that Ramirez employed the M.O. that would become his calling card. The killing of male victims held no significance for him. His methodology called for dispatching the man as quickly as possible, allowing him to indulge his vile fantasies with the woman.

Six weeks after the Zazzara homicides, Ramirez returned to Monterey Park, the scene of the Tsia-Lian Yu murder. This time, he broke into the home of Harold and Jean Wu, shooting the 66-year-old Mr. Wu through the head, before brutally savaging Mrs. Wu, 63, with his fists. Ramirez demanded money and after he got what he wanted, he dragged the frail Jean Wu to the bed and raped her, before fleeing the scene.

Two weeks later he broke into the home that Ruth Wilson, 41, shared with her 12-year-old son. Using threats of violence against the boy, he raped and sodomized Mrs. Wilson, before fleeing. She was later able to provide police with a description - her attacker had been tall, with long dark hair, and of Hispanic origin.

By this time, the media was awash with stories of a serial killer running loose in the city, sparking widespread panic. There was a run on new locks and security systems. Police were on high alert. None of this seems to have bothered Ramirez. Instead of slowing down, his reign of terror was escalating.

On May 29, he attacked Malvia Keller, 83, and her sister Blanche Wolfe, 80, beating the two old ladies so severely with a hammer that the handle broke. A month later, on June 27, he raped a six-year-old girl in Arcadia. A day after that, he murdered 32-year-old Patty Elaine Higgins in her Arcadia home. Five days later he committed another murder in Arcadia, slitting the throat of 75-year-old Mary Louise Cannon. And he surfaced again in Arcadia on July 5, savagely bludgeoning 16-year-old Deidre Palmer with a tire iron. She survived her injuries.

Two days later he was back in Monterey Park, where he battered 61-year-old Joyce Nelson to death with a blunt object. Later that same night he entered the home of 63-year-old Linda Fortuna. He tried to rape her but couldn't get an erection. Then, when Mrs. Fortuna started to scream, he fled, leaving her unharmed.

On July 20, the Night Stalker switched his attention to Glendale, killing and mutilating Maxson Kneiling and his wife Lela, both 66. Perhaps, due to his failure to perform sexually with Mrs. Kneiling, Ramirez carried out another attack that same night. Chitat Assawahem, 32, was shot as he slept. His wife Sakima, 29, was raped, forced into performing oral sex, and then beaten. Ramirez then ransacked the house, netting $30,000 in cash and jewelry. Before he fled, he sodomized the couple's eight-year-old son.

By now, Ramirez had a well-established M.O. and he used it again on August 6, breaking into the home of Christopher and Virginia Petersen. However, in this case, the killer had taken on more than he could handle. Despite the bullet lodged in his brain, Christopher Petersen, a powerfully built man, chased the intruder from his home. Miraculously, Mr. Petersen survived the bullet wound.

Ramirez had more success two nights later, in Diamond Bar, California. Ahmed Zia, 35, was shot in the head and killed while he slept. His wife, Suu Kyi Zia was subjected to a prolonged attack during which she was raped, sodomized and forced to perform oral sex.

Then, with police attention in Los Angeles County intensifying, the Night Stalker shifted his attention north.

Peter and Barbara Pan were attacked on August 18, in Lake Merced, a San Francisco suburb. Mr. Pan was pronounced dead at the scene, his wife survived, but would be an invalid for the rest of her life. San Francisco police immediately caught a break in the case - a man matching the Stalker's description had sold a pair of cufflinks to a pawnbroker. The jewelry turned out to belong to Mr. Pan.

But while police were following this lead, Ramirez was already heading south. On August 24, he attacked a young couple in Mission Viejo, fifty miles south of Los Angeles. Following his now familiar M.O., he shot the man in the head and then proceeded to rape and sodomize the woman before ransacking the house.

However, Ramirez had made his first mistake. Earlier that evening a teenager had noticed an orange Toyota cruising the neighborhood. The behavior of the driver struck the boy as suspicious, so he jotted down the license plate number. Next morning, when news of the attack came out, he passed the license number on to police.

The vehicle turned out to have been stolen from L.A.'s Chinatown district and police were able to lift a print from it, a print that belonged to Richard Ramirez. Police now had a name and photograph of their suspect, and they immediately released it to the media. But could they stop him before he killed again?

With his face being broadcast on TV and in the newspapers you might have thought Ramirez would lay low for a while. However, a week after the Mission Viejo attack, Ramirez tried to steal a car in East L.A., a largely Hispanic area of Los Angeles. Unfortunately for Ramirez, the owner was lying under the car at the time, working on the transmission. The man gave chase and, along with several of his neighbors, managed to apprehend Ramirez, beating him severely and holding him until the police arrived.

Ramirez was charged with fourteen murders and thirty-one other felonies.

His trial would be a protracted and, at times, bizarre affair that ran to almost four years due to multiple delays and arguments over a change of venue and jury selection. The proceedings themselves were typified by squabbles between defense and prosecution attorneys that almost came to blows, by histrionic outbursts from the defendant, and by the attendance in court of a growing band of female "murder groupies." One of the jurors was even murdered during the course of the trial, in an unrelated incident.

Eventually, on September 20, 1989, after almost two months of deliberation, the jury pronounced Ramirez guilty. Two weeks later, on October 3, 1989, they voted for the death penalty on all counts.

Richard Ramirez seemed unmoved by the sentence and was led from the courtroom smiling. "Big Deal," he was heard to say. "Death always went with the territory. I'll see you in Disneyland."

Richard Ramirez died at Marin General Hospital in Greenbrae, California, on June 7, 2013. Cause of death was given as complications due to B-cell lymphoma. He was 53 years old and had been on death row for more than 23 years.

Gary Ridgeway

The Green River Killer

"... she thinks, 'Oh, this guy cares'... which I didn't. I just want to get her in the vehicle and eventually kill her." - Gary Ridgeway

On August 15, 1982, Robert Ainsworth was navigating south along the Green River toward the Seattle's city limits. It was a trip he had made often in his rubber raft, and one that he enjoyed. Along a stretch of the river, Ainsworth saw a couple of men fishing from the bank and exchanged a few words with them as he passed. A short while later, he saw what he believed to be a mannequin floating in the water. He attempted to snag the figure with a pole but overstretched and capsized the raft, pitching himself into the river. It was only then that Ainsworth realized that the figure was not a mannequin, but a dead woman. Seconds later he saw another floating corpse, and struck out for the bank in panicked strokes. Pulling himself ashore, Ainsworth looked desperately for help. He spotted a man and two children on bicycles and ran towards them. Telling the man about his gruesome discovery, he asked him to call the police. Before long, a single policeman arrived at the scene and questioned Ainsworth. Then Ainsworth pointed out to the officer where the corpses lay bobbing with the current, captured between some rocks. The officer immediately called for backup.

Soon the area was sealed off and detectives began searching for evidence, turning up a third corpse in the process. Unlike the other two girls, this one was found in a grassy area about 30 feet from the water. A pair of blue pants was knotted around her neck indicating that she'd been strangled. Bruises on her body suggested that she'd put up a brave, but ultimately futile, fight. She was later identified as Opal Mills, a 16-year-old prostitute. She had been murdered within 24 hours of discovery.

The other two victims were also prostitutes - Marcia Chapman, 31, and Cynthia Hinds, 17. Like Mills, they'd been strangled, but their bodies carried an additional, enigmatic, clue. Each woman had a pyramid-shaped stone inserted into her vagina. Chapman, who'd been reported missing two weeks earlier, had been dead for over a week; Hinds had been killed in the last few days.

The three bodies were not the only ones to be found in the vicinity of the Green River in recent times. Just a few days earlier, the strangled corpse of Seattle prostitute, Deborah Bonner, had been discovered on the riverbank. A month before, Wendy Lee Coffield was found strangled and floating in the water. Six months prior to that horrific discovery, Leanne Wilcox (a friend of Coffield) was found several miles from the river in an empty lot.

The Wilcox murder was initially not connected to the others but nonetheless, Seattle police were in no doubt that they had a serial killer on their hands. They also knew that, unless they caught him soon, more women were going to show up dead. A special task force was therefore assembled to investigate the Green River murders. Headed by Major Richard Kraske, the head of the Criminal Investigation Division, and Detective Dave Reichert of the King County Major Crime Squad, the team also enlisted the help of the FBI's renowned profiler, John Douglas, and veteran investigator Bob Keppel, famous for his ground-breaking work on the Ted Bundy case, nearly a decade earlier.

Almost immediately, the task force was under pressure, swamped by a deluge of information that they had no hope of keeping up with. They simply did not have the means to process the ever-increasing amount of data, resulting in valuable evidence being misplaced, lost or simply overlooked. Eventually, the situation got so bad that the police had to enlist the help of civilian volunteers.

However, some patterns did emerge. The victims were all prostitutes and many of them were known to each other due to working Seattle's infamous 'strip' from   South 139th Street to South 272nd Street. Investigators therefore focused their attention on this area, conducting hundreds of interviews. Despite their obvious fear of the killer, though, many of the streetwalkers were reluctant to speak to the police.

One of the prostitutes did speak, providing details of a man who'd made reference to the Green River murders after he'd raped her. The police began searching for the assailant and announced an arrest on August 20, 1982. But this would prove the first of many false dawns. The man was charged with the rape but cleared of any involvement in the murders.

Another suspect emerged after two prostitutes, Susan Widmark, 21, and Debra Estes, 15, reported being raped at gunpoint by a middle-aged man driving a blue and white pickup truck. Following up on leads provided by the two women, the police arrested Charles Clinton Clark, a butcher, in September. Like the previous suspect, Clark was charged with rape, but provided solid alibis for the times of the Green River murders. Investigators had been dubious of Clark as a suspect anyway, as he'd turned his victims loose after assaulting them.

And this belief proved well founded. While Clark was being booked for the Widmark and Estes rapes, another woman went missing. Mary Bridgett Meehan was 19 years old and 8-months pregnant when she went for a walk and disappeared near the Western Six Motel, close to the Green River Killer's hunting ground.

Meanwhile, a new suspect emerged, a 44-year-old out-of-work taxi driver who was one of the civilian volunteers working with the task force. Detective Dave Reichert first began focusing on this suspect because he so closely fit the profile prepared by John Douglas. The FBI agent believed the killer would be a confident, yet impulsive, middle-aged man who had a good knowledge of the area, had an interest in police work and might try to involve himself in the investigation. He felt the killer would also have strong religious convictions.

The taxi driver fit all of these criteria and he was duly placed under surveillance and eventually brought in for questioning. He vigorously denied having anything to do with the Green River murders and with no solid evidence (other than the fact that he knew five of the victims), the police had to release him.

On September 26, 1982, the decomposing corpse of 17-year-old prostitute, Gisele Lovvorn, was found near some abandoned houses south of Sea-Tac International Airport. She had been strangled to death with a pair of men's black socks. Although her body was found far from the river, the police believed that she was yet another victim of the serial killer they sought.

And the killer was accelerating. Between September 1982 and April 1983, another 14 women, most of them prostitutes, disappeared from the strip. Among the missing; Mary Meehan, Debra Estes, Denise Bush, Shawnda Summers, Shirley Sherrill, Rebecca Marrero, Colleen Brockman, Alma Smith, Delores Williams, Gail Matthews, Andrea Childers, Sandra Gabbert, Kimi-Kai Pitsor and Marie Malvar.

The Marie Malvar murder would provide police with a valuable lead. On April 30, 1983, Malvar's boyfriend saw her talking to a man in a dark-colored truck. The two of them appeared to be engaged in an argument, but in the next moment, the truck sped off with Malvar inside. Suspicious, the boyfriend followed, but lost the truck in traffic. When Malvar failed to return, he reported the incident to the police.

Less than a week later, the boyfriend, along with Malvar's father and brother, spotted the truck again, near the spot where he'd lost it. They followed the vehicle to a house on South 348th Street, then reported the address to the police. Officers called on the property and spoke with the owner, Gary Ridgeway. He denied knowing Malvar and the police had no reason to disbelieve him.

A dark truck was also mentioned in connection with the April disappearance of a young prostitute named Kimi-Kai Pitsor. Pitsor's pimp saw her getting into a dark green pickup driven by a man with a pockmarked face. When Pitsor failed to return, the pimp reported her disappearance to police, but no connection was made between this incident and that involving Marie Malvar.

By the spring of 1983, the Green River investigation was at a standstill. All of the suspects that had been considered had by now been cleared and, despite the fact that prostitutes were continuing to disappear from the streets, there were no new leads. The task force was drowning in paperwork, unable to cope with the avalanche of tips being called in daily. In desperation, they turned to Bob Keppel for help.

In late April, Keppel spent three weeks going over all the available information on the Green River murders. He then compiled a damning report, criticizing the task force for its chaotic approach to the investigation. He recommended a complete reorganization of all the available data in order to uncover patterns between the various murders, which would hopefully provide indicators to the killer's identity.

It wasn't exactly what King's County officials were hoping to hear. The search for the Green River Killer had already escalated into the biggest and most expensive manhunt in US history. The changes Keppel was suggesting would push the cost of the investigation over $2 million. Still, they had no choice. The killer was still out there, and he was still killing.

On May 8, 1983, the body of Carol Ann Christensen, 21, was discovered by a family searching for mushrooms in a wooded area near Maple Valley. The corpse was bizarrely displayed, a brown paper bag over her head, a dead fish placed on her shoulder, another on her left breast, a bottle between her legs and some ground beef in her left hand. If it were not for a familiar Green River calling card, the police might have thought this was not connected to their series. Christensen had a pyramid shaped stone inserted in her vagina.

During the spring and summer of 1983, nine more young women – Martina Authorlee, Cheryl Lee Wims, 18, Yvonne Antosh, 19, Carrie Rois, 15, Constance Naon, 21, Tammie Liles, 16, Keli McGuiness, 18, Tina Thompson, 22, and April Buttram, 17 – disappeared, most of them believed to be victims of the Green River Killer.

And bodies kept turning up, too. In June of '83, the unidentified remains of a young woman were found on SW Tualatin Road; on August 11, the body of Shawnda Summers was discovered near the Sea-Tac Airport; a day later another unidentified corpse was found at the Sea-Tac Airport North site.

And still, the carnage continued. September to December 1983 produced nine more disappearances and the discovery of seven more decomposing corpses. The missing women, were Debbie Abernathy, 26, Tracy Ann Winston, 19, Patricia Osborn, Maureen

Feeney, Mary Sue Bello, 25, Pammy Avent, 16, Delise Plager, 22, Kim Nelson, 26, and Lisa Lorraine Yates.

Those whose bodies were discovered included Delores Williams, 17, and Gail Matthews, 23, both found at Star Lake. On October 15, the skeletal remains of Yvonne Antosh were found near Soos Creek on Auburn-Black Diamond Road. Twelve days later, the partially buried skeleton of Constance Naon turned up in an area south of Sea-Tac Airport.

In January 1984, the Green River Task Force had a new leader, with Captain Frank Adamson, formerly of the police department's Internal Affairs unit, taking over the reins. Adamson made some drastic changes, including relocating task force headquarters to Burien County, which was near the airport and closer to the murderer's killing ground. He also implemented many of Bob Keppel's recommendations. One of those was to reduce the suspect list, categorizing suspects according to their likelihood of being the Green River Killer, and removing marginal suspects. This allowed investigators to focus more intently on a smaller pool of candidates.

The new year started with no new discoveries, but on February 14, 1984, the skeletal remains of a woman (later identified as Denise Louise Plager) were found beside I-90, some 40 miles from Seattle. Over the next two months, another nine bodies were found including Cheryl Wims, 18, Lisa Yates, 26, Debbie Abernathy, Terry Milligan, 16, Sandra Gabbert, 17, and Alma Smith, 22.

Despite a perceived lack of progress by the Green River Task Force, the investigation was advancing, albeit slowly. For example, the team had determined that the corpses were being distributed over a series of dumpsites and that there was usually some effort to conceal them. Many of the bodies had been left at illegal waste dumping areas and FBI profiler John Douglas believed that this was significant. It indicated that the killer regarded his victims as "human garbage."

The killer had also shifted his dumpsites over time. Beginning in and around the Green River, he'd shifted to Sea-Tac Airport and Star Lake, then to areas in the vicinity of Mountain View Cemetery and North Bend. In addition, it was determined that he was picking his victims from two primary areas, the strip, and downtown Seattle.

The task force believed that the killer worked or lived close to the area where he was dumping the bodies. These areas formed a roughly triangular shape and investigators were certain that he lived somewhere within that triangle.

In April, an important piece of evidence was found at one of the dumpsites, a shoe print which indicated that the killer wore size 10 or 11 shoes. Although this got investigators no closer to catching their killer, it would be important for comparison purposes if, and when, the man was apprehended.

A less conventional piece of information turned up later that same month. Barbara Kubik-Pattern, one of the task force volunteers and a self-styled psychic, informed investigators that she'd had a vision of where a woman's body could be found, close to Interstate 90. Frustrated that the police wouldn't take her tip-off seriously, Kubik-Pattern conducted her own search and eventually found the body.

The decomposing remains were of Amina Agisheff, 36, who had disappeared on her way to work on July 7, 1982. Unlike most of the other victims, Agisheff was not a prostitute. Nonetheless, investigators believed that she was another victim of the Green River Killer, more than likely one of his earliest kills.

On May 26, two children playing on Jovita Road in Pierce County were shocked to find a skeleton. The remains turned out to belong to Colleen Brockman, a 15-year-old runaway. Task force investigators believed that there were probably more bodies to be found in that area, so they carried out an extensive search, with the assistance of a team of teenaged Boy Scouts. The search eventually bore fruit when one of the scouts discovered skeletal remains concealed under some trash. The remains were later identified as 22-year-old Kelly Ware.

It was now three years since the Green River Killer had announced his deadly presence and yet the police were no closer to tracking him. On November 13, the badly decomposed remains of Mary Meehan and her unborn baby were found buried beneath an empty lot, south of Sea-Tac. Meehan was the only victim to be fully buried by the killer.

On December 15, the skull of Kimi-Kai Pitsor was found near Mountain View Cemetery.

Two weeks later, the Green River Task Force increased by more than half. The force was coming under increasing official and public pressure to catch the killer, but even as they intensified their efforts, he appeared to be slowing down. The murders would still continue for some time, but the frantic pace of disappearances and gruesome discoveries would never again reach 1982/83 levels.

In August 1984, investigators believed they had a big break in the case when two criminals in a San Francisco jail confessed to the Green River murders. However, after extensive interviews, the confessions were determined to be a hoax.

Several months later, the Task Force received an offer of help from an unusual source. Ted Bundy, arguably America's most notorious serial killer, then on death row in Florida, offered to assist Bob Keppel in catching the killer. Bundy believed he could offer Keppel a unique insight into the murderer's thinking and it was an offer Keppel couldn't turn down. Over the course of a number of letters, Keppel asked detailed questions of Bundy. Although Bundy's input did not lead Keppel to the killer, they provided some valuable information, especially the idea that the killer befriended the victims in order to convince them to go with him (this turned out to be true). Bundy also backed up Keppel's belief that the killer's home would be within the area mapped out by his dump sites.

Between October and December 1984, two more bodies, Mary Sue Bello, 25, and Martina Authorlee, 18, were discovered, both near Highway 410. The total body count now stood at 31, although only 28 of those made it onto the official Green River list. Fourteen women were still missing. On March 10, 1985, another partially buried body was found near Star Lake Road. The victim was Carrie Rois, 15, missing since the summer of 1983.

In mid-June, the skeletal remains of two more women were discovered near Tigard, Oregon. Despite this being far from the Green River Killer's territory, police recovered enough evidence from the scene to attribute the murders to him. The victims were later identified as Seattle prostitutes Denise Bush, 23, and Shirley Sherrill, 19.

Meanwhile, FBI profiler John Douglas had re-evaluated his previous profile and decided that the police were, in fact, looking for two separate killers, one who made an effort to conceal his kills and another who left his victims' bodies openly exposed to detection. The idea seemed plausible, but at this time the task force did not have a single viable suspect, let alone two.

Winter brought the discovery of yet another three sets of remains, Mary West, Kimi-Kai Pitsor, and an unidentified white female. Pitsor's skull had actually been found at Mountain View Cemetery in December 1983, leaving detectives to ponder how her body had ended up in a different location. With animal activity ruled out, it was deemed to be an attempt by the killer to taunt the police.

In February 1986, a spokesman for the Task Force announced that they were questioning a "person of interest." It seemed like a genuine break had been made in the case. However, as with previous suspects, the man was soon released, resulting in the force being subjected to even more pressure. The media was particularly scathing, describing the Green River Task Force as a "joke."

Three more skeletonized corpses were discovered during the summer, all of them off I-90, east of Seattle. The victims were Maureen Feeney, 19, Kim Nelson, 26, and another, unidentifiable, young woman.

The death toll by now was heading rapidly towards 40. Despite this, budget constraints and the lack of any new leads led to the task force being cut by half, towards the end of 1986. There was also a new man in charge, with Captain James Pompey taking over from Frank Adamson. He'd no sooner taken over his post than two more bodies were discovered. This time, the dumpsite was in an area north of Vancouver, British Columbia. Yet, the police had no doubt that the murders were the work of the Green River Killer, not least because the partial remains of other victims were scattered alongside the bodies of the two women.

In the beginning months of 1987, investigators had a new suspect. The man had previously been picked up in May 1984 after trying to solicit an undercover police officer posing as a prostitute. At that time he'd been released after passing a polygraph. Looking deeper into the suspect's past, though, investigators learned that he'd once been arrested for choking a prostitute near the Sea-Tac International Airport. He'd claimed self-defense and been released without charge. That had been in 1980. In 1982, he'd been questioned after being found with a prostitute in his truck. Then, in 1983, he'd again been questioned regarding the disappearance of prostitute Marie Malvar. His name was Gary Ridgeway and the more task force Detective Haney looked at him, the more he believed he might be the Green River Killer.

Haney learned from Ridgeway's ex-wife that he often frequented the dumpsites where many of the bodies had been found. He also found that Ridgeway passed the strip every day on his way to work and that he had regularly been seen cruising the area between 1982 and 1983, at the height of the murders. Perhaps most damaging, it was found that Ridgeway was absent or off duty from work on every occasion that a victim disappeared.

On April 8, 1987, the police obtained a warrant and searched Ridgeway's house. They also took blood and hair samples for comparison with evidence from the Green River victims. However, there was insufficient evidence to arrest him and Ridgeway was released.

Several weeks after Ridgeway's release, Captain James Pompey suffered a massive heart attack related to a scuba-diving accident. Pompey's death was seized on by the press, who suggested that he had been murdered by the Green River Killer. The farfetched theory was that the killer was a police officer and had murdered Pompey to avoid detection. Pompey was replaced by Captain Greg Boyle.

In June, three boys out hunting for aluminum cans discovered the skeletal remains of a young woman, later identified as Cindy Ann Smith, 17. She had been missing for approximately three years.

More remains turned up over the following year, including those of 14-year-old runaway Debbie Gonzales, and prostitute Debra Estes, 15, who had disappeared six years earlier. These deaths were attributed to the Green River Killer but while bodies continued to be discovered, there had been no recent murders and the police began to believe that the killer had left the Seattle area, was dead, or was perhaps in prison on some other charge.

In October 1989, the skeletal remains of Andrea Childers were found in a vacant lot near Star Lake. In February 1990, the skull of Denise Bush was found in a wooded area in Southgate Park in Tukwila, Washington. The remainder of Bush's body had been found in Oregon five years earlier.

More reductions in task force personnel over the next two years saw the force reduced to just a single investigator by July 1991. There was a genuine belief among law officers that the Green River Killer would never be caught. Nine years of investigative work and $15 million later, they were no closer to catching the elusive killer. It seemed the Green River murders would remain as one of the great, unsolved murder mysteries. And so it remained over the next decade.

In April 2001, Detective Dave Reichert, one of the original investigators on the case, decided to re-open the investigation. It was 20 years since the first murder, and Reichert had in the interim become sheriff of King County. The intervening years had not dimmed his determination to catch the Green River Killer, and this time, he believed he had the technology to do it.

Reichert formed a new 30-member task force that included DNA and forensic experts. He called for all evidence to be re-examined and for forensic evidence to be sent to the labs for testing. Among those samples was semen taken from three victims – Opal Mills, Marcia Chapman, and Carol Christensen. Subjected to DNA analysis, they returned a match to the task force's main suspect from 1987 – Gary Ridgeway. The news that they'd finally caught the killer reportedly reduced Reichert to tears.

On November 30, Ridgeway was intercepted on his way home from work and arrested on four counts of aggravated murder. The man that investigators had sought for 20 years was finally in custody.

Born in Salt Lake City, Utah, on February 18, 1949, Ridgeway was a thrice-married spray painter who was said by his ex-wives to have an insatiable sexual appetite. Neighbors said that he appeared obsessed with prostitutes and complained constantly about them conducting business in his neighborhood. He was also deeply religious, a regular churchgoer who was said by his current wife to sometimes cry while reading the bible.

On November 5, 2003, Gary Ridgeway, then aged 54, admitted to the murders of 48 women, most of whom were killed between 1982 and 1984. The confession was part of a plea bargain in terms of which Ridgeway would avoid the death penalty and accept 48 life sentences without the possibility of parole.

He is currently serving those sentences at Washington State Penitentiary in Walla Walla.

What Makes A Serial Killer?

"I don't march to the same drummer you do." – Convicted killer Douglas Clark a.k.a. The Sunset Strip Slayer

What makes a serial killer? Is there something unique in their genetic make-up, their physiology, thought patterns, or upbringing? Do they lack morality or social programming? Are they unable to control their rage and sexual urges? Are they mad or bad? What sets them apart?

These questions have vexed criminologists, profilers, psychologists, and forensic psychiatrists for decades. They've been the subject of countless studies and dissertations. They've formed the basis of thousands of man-hours worth of interviews and investigation. And yet, definitive answers remain elusive.

Serial killers themselves have offered some suggestions. Henry Lee Lucas blamed his upbringing; Jeffrey Dahmer said that he was born with a part of him missing; Ted Bundy blamed pornography; Herbert Mullin, said it was voices in his head ordering him to kill; Kenneth Bianchi blamed an alter-ego, while Bobby Joe Long said a motorcycle accident turned him into a serial sex killer. Some, like John Wayne Gacy, even had the temerity to blame their victims.

As for the rest of us, we console ourselves that they must be insane. After all, what sane person could slaughter another for pleasure? What normal person could perpetuate the atrocities that serial killers do, and repeat them again and again?

Yet the most terrifying thing about serial killers is that they are not shambling, jabbering ogres, but rational and calculating, impossible to tell from the general populace until it's too late.

So what exactly is a serial killer?

The National Institutes of Justice define serial murder as;

"A series of two or more murders committed as separate events, usually, but not always, by one offender acting alone. The crimes may occur over a period of time, ranging from hours to years. Quite often the motive is psychological, and the offender's behavior and the physical evidence observed at the crime scene will reflect sadistic sexual overtones."

And the FBI's Behavioral Science Unit provides us with some traits common in serial killers.

- They are typically white males in their twenties and thirties.
- They are usually quite smart, with an IQ designated, "bright normal."
- Despite their intelligence, they are underachievers, often doing poorly at school, and ending up in unskilled employment.
- They often come from broken homes with an absent father and domineering mother. Some are adopted. Often, there is

a history of psychiatric problems, criminality, and substance abuse in their families.

- Many were physically, psychological, and/or sexually abused in childhood. Some have suffered head trauma due to abuse or accident.
- In adolescence, many of them wet the bed, started fires, and tortured animals.
- They have problems with male authority figures and strong hostility towards women.
- They manifest psychological problems at an early age. Many have spent time in institutions as children.
- They have a general hatred towards humanity, including themselves. Some report suicidal thoughts as teenagers.
- They display an interest in sex at an unnaturally young age. As they mature this interest becomes obsessive and turns towards fetishism, voyeurism, and violent pornography.

A Façade of Normality

The traits listed above might incline you to believe that you'd be able to spot a serial killer a mile off, but the frightening truth is that they are masters at camouflage, deceit, and deception. They know exactly how to blend in, how to avert your suspicions, how to put you at ease. They are the charming stranger who strikes up a conversation with you on the bus, the lost driver who courteously asks for directions, the man hobbling on a cane who politely asks for your help.

Like all skilled predators, they can sniff out the slightest hint of an opportunity, they know who to target and how to stalk. Being psychologically vacant they are adept at assuming whatever role they need, and that role will be the one required to snare their victim. To quote serial killer, Henry Lee Lucas, "it's like being a movie star... you're just playing the part."

Is serial murder a recent phenomenon?

Since we're trying to understand what makes a serial killer, this is a valid question, and the answer depends who you're listening to, because there are two distinct schools of thought. One believes that societal influences since just before the turn of the 20th century (and especially since WWII) have created the perfect conditions for the emergence of serial killers. They point to serial killers as a symptom of crowded rat syndrome, a product of class struggle and a manifestation of our attitudes towards sex.

The only problem with this argument is that it suggests that serial killers are purely a product of their environment. I consider that unlikely and am more inclined towards the second hypothesis, which holds that serial killers have always lived among us.

Adherents to this belief point to acts of human barbarism throughout history, from the terrible legends that appear in folklore, to the crimes of Gilles de Rais and Elizabeth Bathory, to the vicious outlaws and desperados of the Old West. They regard tales of werewolves, vampires, and man-eating trolls, as attempts by our less sophisticated ancestors to make sense of the hideous crimes committed by historical serial killers. A number of these legendary monsters, like the German "werewolf" Peter Stubbe and his French counterpart, Gilles Garnier, were in fact captured and put to death. They proved to be, not lycanthropes, but all too human monsters, serial killers, in fact.

What makes a serial killer?

No single cause will ever provide an answer as to why serial killers are driven to commit murder again and again. Rather a combination of factors, physiological, psychological, and environmental, must be in play. Nonetheless, we can look at the known commonalities in captured serial killers and draw some conclusions. Is this a comprehensive list? Hardly. We simply don't have the knowledge to solve the enigma of the serial killer.

Psychopaths

All serial killers, except perhaps for the small minority that are genuinely psychotic, are psychopaths. They would not be able to commit their horrendous crimes otherwise. Psychopaths are characterized by their irrationally antisocial behavior, their lack of conscience, their emotional emptiness, and their appetite for risk, all of which could easily be applied to serial killers.

Lacking in empathy, they have no problem in turning their victims into objects, there to be exploited and manipulated. Being devoid of emotions (in the way that you and I would understand them) they are like a blank screen, onto which can be projected whatever suits their needs in the moment. This is what makes them so good at play acting and manipulation.

Being compulsive thrill seekers, they are literally fearless, sometimes abducting victims in broad daylight, or with clear risk of discovery. This thrill seeking behavior also means that they are less easily stimulated than normal people. They require higher levels of excitement to get their rocks off, even if it means murder and mayhem.

Does this mean that all psychopaths become serial killers? Absolutely not. Most psychopaths aren't even criminals. In fact, many excel in fields like business and political leadership. Not all psychopaths are serial killers, but all serial killers, most certainly, are psychopaths.

Sexual Deviance

A second factor that must be present in all serial killers is sexual deviance. Serial murders are by their nature, sex crimes. A sexual motive is a requisite in both the Institutes of Justice and FBI definitions and an examination of any serial murder (even those that appear to have a different motive) will undoubtedly prove that the killer achieved some form of sexual release in the commission of the crime.

According to Ressler, Burgess, and Douglas in Sexual Homicide: Patterns and Motives, there are two types of sexual homicide: "the rape or displaced anger murder" and the "sadistic, or lust murder."

For some murderers, the rape is the primary objective for the crime, the murder committed to cover it up. For others, the act of murder and the ritual acts associated with it, provide the sexual release. The annals of serial murder abound with such cases, Bundy, Kearney, Kemper, Nilsen and others were necrophiles; Rader, Kraft, Berdella et al. achieved sexual release through torture; others like Kroll and Fish, through cannibalism. Still others are aroused by stabbing or by the "intimate" act of strangulation.

And with serial killers this deviance usually manifests in childhood. Fledgling serial killers are often flashers, peeping toms, molesters of younger children, chronic masturbators, even, as in the case of Harvey Glatman, juvenile sadomasochists. And even if they're not committing sex crimes at a young age, they're thinking about them.

Other Common Factors

But even a psychopath with unusual sexual appetites won't necessarily become a serial killer. He might find a partner (or more likely, partners) to cater for his tastes, or he might visit prostitutes who will do the same for a price. He may turn his talents towards becoming a 'love 'em and leave 'em' pick-up artist.

No, something else needs to happen to push our young psychopath over the threshold. An additional X-factor, or factors, needs to be in place. Thanks to the work done by the FBI in interviews with captured serial murderers, we know what some of those factors are.

Born Bad

The idea that someone might be inherently evil would have been scoffed at not too long ago. However, as we begin to understand more about the unique reality that murderers inhabit, it becomes clear that their warped view of the world takes root at an early age.

"Trash Bag Killer" Patrick Kearney said that he knew from age 8 that he would kill people; Ed Kemper had a crush on his second grade teacher, but told a friend, "if I kiss her I would have to kill her first"; Ted Bundy was leaving butcher's knives in his aunt's bed at the age of just 3; John Joubert was slashing girls with a razor blade before he reached his teens; Harvey Glatman was practicing sadomasochism when he was only 4 years old.

Child Abuse

Not every abused child becomes a serial killer, but a disproportionately high number of serial killers suffered abuse as children. "Boston Strangler," Albert De Salvo's father was a particularly brutal man who regularly beat his wife and children with metal pipes, brought prostitutes home and even sold his children into slavery. Joseph Kallinger's mother forced him to hold his hand over a flame, and beat him if he cried. Henry Lee Lucas' mother beat him so hard she fractured his skull. She also forced the young boy to watch her having sex with men.

And yet, others serial killers grew up in seemingly normal homes - Jeffrey Dahmer, for example, or Joel Rifkin, or Patrick Kearney.

Some, like "Pied Piper of Tucson," Charles Schmid, were even pampered and indulged, their every desire catered to.

Domineering Mothers

Many serial killers seem to come from a home with an absent or passive father figure, and a dominating mother. This was certainly the case with both Henry Lee Lucas and Ed Kemper, both of whom eventually murdered their mothers.

Joseph Kallinger's mother was a sadist; Ed Gein's a religious nut who constantly warned him of the dangers of sex. Bobby Joe Long's mother made him sleep in her bed until he was thirteen. Ed Kemper's mom locked him in the cellar because she said his large size frightened his sisters. Charles Manson's mother reportedly traded him for a pitcher of beer. And at the other end of the scale was "Hillside Strangler" Kenneth Bianchi's cloyingly overprotective mom.

Either way, dysfunctional mother/son relationships seem to be present in the upbringing of an alarmingly high number of serial killers.

Adoption

Millions of children are adopted every year and grow up to live normal, productive lives. But there are an unusually high percentage of serial killers who were given up by their birth

mothers for adoption. David Berkowitz, Charles Schmid, Joel
Rifkin, Kenneth Bianchi, and Joseph Kallinger (to name a few) all
fall into this category.

Finding out that one was adopted can be devastating for any child,
creating a sense of disconnect, an uncertainty over one's identity.
And, in a child already suffering with other issues (such as some of
those mentioned above), it can be particularly devastating,
unleashing feelings of rejection and simmering anger.

Exposure to Violence

Some serial killers blame juvenile exposure to violence for their
misdeeds. Ed Gein, for example, claimed that seeing farm animals
slaughtered gave him perverted ideas, while both Albert Fish and
Andrei Chikatilo blamed their brutal murders on frightening
stories they were told as children. As a child, John George Haigh
saw a man decapitated by a bomb during the London blitz in
WWII. Richard Ramirez was only thirteen when his cousin
committed a murder right in front of him (those who knew him at
the time said he showed no emotion and continued to idolize his
cousin).

Rejection by Peers

Many serial killers are outsiders and loners in childhood. The
nerdy Joel Rifkin was picked on and bullied throughout his school

years. Likewise, the diminutive and sickly Patrick Kearney. Henry Lee Lucas was ridiculed and ostracized because of his glass eye, Kenneth Bianchi because of his incontinence. Jeffrey Dahmer was deliberately antisocial as a kid, a teenaged alcoholic who laughed when he saw a classmate injured. Harvey Glatman preferred spending time alone in his room indulging in autoerotic strangulation.

Separated from their peers, these troubled youngsters begin to rely on fantasy to bridge the gap. Often these begin as "revenge fantasies" against those who have wronged them, like abusive parents or schoolyard bullies. The relief that these fantasies bring, leads to ever more violent daydreams, which may begin to manifest through two of the three "triad" behaviors, fire-starting and animal cruelty.

Fantasy

The role of fantasy in the metamorphosis of a killer has been extensively studied. All of us fantasize at some time, perhaps about asking a pretty girl out, or meeting our favorite celebrity or turning out for our favorite sports teams. The fantasies of a fledgling serial killer, though, are a deep and disturbing mix of murder, mutilation, and aberrant sex.

Serial killers will dwell on these fantasies (sometimes for years), deepening them and adding layers of detail. Eventually though, the fantasy will no longer be enough and they'll feel compelled to act, the pressure building until it is impossible to resist.

How long before fantasy manifests in reality? Peter Kurten, Jesse Pomeroy, and Mary Bell committed multiple murders as children, Yosemite killer, Cary Stayner, said that he'd fantasized about killing a woman for 30 years before he eventually followed through.

Brain Damage

Brain damage, especially to the hypothalamus, limbic region, and temporal lobe can cause severe behavioral changes, specifically as regards emotion, empathy, and aggression responses.

Many serial killers - Leonard Lake, David Berkowitz, Kenneth Bianchi, John Wayne Gacy, Carl Panzram, Henry Lee Lucas, Bobby Joe Long, among them - have suffered head injuries, either in accidents or in childhood beatings.

Others, Ted Bundy for example, have been subjected to extensive X-rays and brain scans, which revealed no evidence of brain damage or trauma. Neither does everyone who suffers head trauma become a killer. So while brain damage or dysfunction is undoubtedly a factor in the behavior of some serial killers, it is far from being a universal "kill switch."

Societal Influences

Psychopaths find it difficult to accept responsibility for their actions, so it is unsurprising that many serial killers blame society for their acts. The poster boy for this theory is Ted Bundy. Bundy has spoken at length about the influence of violent pornography on the killer that he became.

Is there any validity to his claims?

We do seem to be a society that glorifies violence, from live footage of bombs falling on Baghdad, to movies in which the hero is every bit as violent as the bad guy he's trying to defeat. Porn, too, is easily available, both online and in movies and magazines. But neither of these provides a rationale for serial murder. If everyone who watched a Rambo movie or downloaded porn was to become a serial killer we'd have an epidemic on our hands.

Conclusion

At the beginning of the article, I asked, "What makes a serial killer?" The reasons may be more complex than we think, perhaps beyond our comprehension. A better question to ask may be, "Is anyone capable of serial murder?" And the answer to that is an emphatic "No!"

The creation of a serial killer requires a perfect (or more appropriately, an imperfect) storm, whereby some of the factors mention above, and perhaps some others that are not, are blended together into a toxic brew with psychopathy and sexual deviance.

A combination of aberrant psychology, childhood abuse, and peer rejection leading to the development of fantasies that involve death and sex and then manifest in fire-starting and animal cruelty can hardly fail to produce someone who, given the opportunity, will kill and kill again.

For more True Crime books by Robert Keller please visit

http://bit.ly/kellerbooks